Sex, Boys & You

Sex, Boys & You

Be Your Own
Best Girlfriend

Joni Arredia

Perc Publishing • Toledo, Ohio

ISBN 0-9653203-2-4
Library of Congress Catalog Number 98-066865

Cover by Kevin Ewing, Ewing Design and Illustration
Interior by Troy Scott Parker, Cimarron Design

Perc Publishing, P.O. Box 351030, Toledo, Ohio 43635
PERC: Personal Energies, Resources, and Capabilities

To my sweet baby girls,
Lauren and Emily

Contents

Acknowledgements

My kindness, strength, generosity and power come from the undying love of my family. My darling Chuck, Lauren and Emily. I am supremely loved. Thank you. You are my greatest dream come true.

DJ, Josie, Mary, Ursula and Rose, my listeners and my comforters. I am with you always.

My Perfect Strangers, Perfect Friends, young women who used some of their energy during the playful days of summer to read an unfinished manuscript. Your red pen editing was thought provoking and honest. You never met me and yet, you took the time to help me. Outstanding! Thank you Stephanie Shnapp, Farah Mokdad, Kortney Shayer, Dahkibra Draper, Nichole Kizer, Sara Rodriquez, Katie Dillard, Candace Harmon and Hollie Harmon.

A heartfelt thank you to other women whom I love and respect. Shirley Hollstein, Christy Wheeler, Maggie Swigart, Carey Geiger, Joan Durgin, Darrah Carr, Alyson Ray, and Polly Weitzel.

Barbara Meyer, my editor, thank you for your brilliance. Barbara Stahl, thank you for my wings.

Now, for the delicious frosting on the cake, The Perc Girls! Kelly Creech and Sharon Naragon. Kelly, I admire your firm balance and silly sense of humor. A lovely mix! Sharon, I love your vision of simplicity and spirit. In two beautiful words, Thank You.

Hello!

Foreword

HI! My name is Joni Arredia, and if you're a teen girl, I've written this book just for you.

It's time you had a book written with *you* in mind: the *you* that's trying to figure out what she's all about; the *you* that can be whatever she dreams of being.

It's a very cool thing to be a girl—if you embrace your *muliebrity* in a positive way! I came upon that fabulous word—*muliebrity* (myoo-lee-EBB-ri-tee)—when I was writing my first book a few years ago. To pronounce *muliebrity,* just say the word celebrity and replace the "cel" with "mule" and add an "e". Now smooth it all out and you can pronounce *muliebrity.* It's defined as "the state of being a woman," "the qualities characteristic of women," or "possessing full womanly powers."

I especially like that last definition, because of the word *powers.* Too often, women feel powerless, and end up being victims. That doesn't have to be the case, however, not if you take the time now to develop your muliebrity.

Never forget that you have the following tremendous powers, girls:

- The power to reach for your dreams.
- The power to determine how you will permit others to treat you.
- The power to become the person you want to be.
- The power to make life happen, instead of having life happen to you.

If you exercise your muliebrity, you need never be a victim of abuse of any kind, be it circumstance, ignorance, discrimination, or violence.

As we go through this book together, I'm going to talk about developing your muliebrity. But, I'm not going to pretend to be your mom. I hope to share what I know without preaching or lecturing my points. I simply want to cradle your thoughts, concerns and fears.

I know that it's hard for you and your mom to talk about some things. It was hard for me, as a girl, too. And, as a mother, I must confess, I'm sure I don't always do such a bang-up job with my own two daughters. I give it my best shot, but sometimes it's hard to find the right words. Other times, I just can't bring myself to talk to my girls about certain things. And there are times that, no matter what I say, my girls figure it's wrong, just because I'm Mom.

I understand that. And I know that my girls will go elsewhere to find answers to their questions. I did. I have no doubt you will, too.

I'm hoping one place you'll turn to is this book: it contains information that many women, like me, never figured out until halfway through life. I'm sure that I would have wanted to figure some of it out on my own, but it would have been terrific to have this stuff tucked away in the back of my brain as food for thought. This book helps during those times when you wonder if you're normal and if being normal is really all that important!

For some of you, reading a book is not on your list of "Things I Love to Do." When I was your age, it wasn't on my list either. However, when I was a teenager, I never had a book like this one—a book that talked about me as a person, as a female, as the kind of woman I could be. A book that asked me what kind of woman I *wanted* to be—**and then inspired me to become it.**

So read just part of this book. Or even all of it. Then read it again. It's quick and easy. And when you're through, pass it along with a smile.

CHAPTER ONE

YOUR TEEN YEARS. THE AGONY AND THE ECSTASY.

It was the best of times,
it was the worst of times.

– Charles Dickens, describing the French Revolution

It was the best of times, it was the worst of times.

– Joni Arredia, describing the teen years

JUST A YEAR AGO, I had absolutely no inkling I'd write a book for teenagers.

At that time, I had just published a book called *Muliebrity: Qualities of a Woman.* That book is all about how women can be happy and live their dreams—no matter what had happened to them in the past. I knew that was true, because I'd made my own journey from horror to happiness. I wanted to share my experience with women everywhere, and when my book hit the stores, I received a lot of positive feedback.

What was fascinating to me about the feedback was how many women—from ages twenty to eighty—said, "I wish I'd known what was in this book when I was a teenager."

Why did all those women say that?

- Some wished they'd dreamed bigger dreams when they were young and then pursued them, instead of settling for less.
- Many regretted the years they'd wasted, unhappy and depressed, just floating through life, rather than taking control of their lives.
- Most said they'd spent way too much of their lives focusing on their weaknesses and limitations rather than on their strengths and talents.

In other words, many grown women wished they'd had better or more information when they started out as adults, so that they could have lived all of their lives the way they wanted to. And here's where we get back to you.

You Can Be Anything You Want to Be

If you're a teen girl today, you're blessed with opportunities your grandmother—and even your mother—didn't have when they were young.

You can be anything you want to be. Nobody—at least no one worth knowing—will look at you funny or treat you like less of a woman because you want to be an astronaut, an inventor, a graphic artist, or even a traditional stay-at-home mom. Nobody will think its weird or unfeminine for you to be a professional athlete and actually sweat in public. In your great-grandmother's time, women would never sweat, and didn't even perspire—they glowed. Yeah, right.

Today, you don't—or shouldn't—have to hide that you're smart in order to get a boyfriend. Girls did that all too often back in the Old Days. If you want a good laugh, dig up copies of *Seventeen* from the 1960s and read the articles on how to attract boys: "Discuss only those subjects that interest him." "Let him do most of the talking." "Never disagree with his opinions." Yikes! Today, if you're more interested in schoolwork, activities, or volunteering than in boys, that's just fine. (For more chuckles from the Dark Ages, see the rules on "How to Be a Good Wife" on page 22.)

Unfortunately, despite today's unlimited opportunities, girls can still end up unhappy and unfulfilled—just as unhappy and unfulfilled as your great-great-grandmother may have been, trapped in the only role society allowed her to play in life. Even with all those opportunities, you've still got to navigate your way through the teen years, and, as you know—being a teen is tough.

Sometimes It's Tough to Be a Teen

For example, just because you can choose to fly a jet fighter some day doesn't mean you can get rid of the zits you've got now or the ones you may still have in your 20s and 30s! Knowing you'll be given an equal chance with men in the future doesn't mean that all the changes your body is going through are going to go away. And, the fact that you just might be elected president in 2025 doesn't provide much comfort if your current crush doesn't know you exist.

It's wonderful to be a teenager, but it's scary, too. You're growing up, making more of your own choices, and finding out who you are. You've got to start thinking about some serious stuff, like what you want to do after high school. You may be interested in guys and dating, but if you're smart, that means you need to sit down and really consider how you plan to deal with issues of sex and intimacy.

Right now, you probably feel you're different from everyone else, and that no one—especially your parents—understands

All women have the potential to be strong.

Your Teen Years. The Agony and the Ecstasy.

what you're thinking or feeling. You may also believe that you've got to please everybody: your parents want you to act one way; your boyfriend, another; and your friends, yet another. And, you have your own ideas about how you want to conduct your life.

I think that it's safe to say that you're never going to go through another seven years in your life that are as confusing or as exciting as adolescence. This is **the** period in your life specifically designed for you to dream, to plan, to think, and to determine who it is you want to be from this time forward. Starting in your teen years, you'll be making choices about the way you live the rest of your life. However, also remember, that your teen choices won't necessarily last forever. As each of us grows up, our likes and dislikes grow up too. You can successfully change careers throughout your life. Just think, at the delicious age of forty, I wrote and published my first book! If you believe it, you can do it!

You Have Control Over Your Life

One of the most important choices you can make is to live your life deliberately. What do I mean by that? You should recognize that the role you play in shaping your life is as large as you choose to make it. You can choose to be in control of your life, to set goals, and to reach for dreams. Or, you can choose to forfeit that control, fail to dream and reach, and simply drift through life as a victim of circumstance.

Part of becoming a strong woman—and all women have the potential to be strong—is realizing that being female does not have to mean being a victim of anything including circumstance, ignorance, discrimination, or abuse. You have control over your life! Our great First Lady, Eleanor Roosevelt, once said, "No one can make you feel inferior without your consent." This can also mean we need to take credit for our mistakes. Owning up to a mistake made is a very good thing! It prevents you from making the same mistake twice. This is strength.

Right now—this very moment—you can begin to learn to live so that life ever after is the glorious, happy, fulfilled existence I honestly believe it was meant to be. As you grapple with the challenges of adolescence, what I'm saying may be hard to believe, but please stick with me. It's true: I know, because I've done it. And in this book, we'll talk about how you can do it, too.

So let's go! Empowerment is just around the corner!

"How to Be a Good Wife"

Recently a friend gave me a list titled "How to Be a Good Wife" from a 1950s home economics book. Back then, girls took Home Ec and boys took Shop, and never the twain did meet. Here are some of the highlights of that list:

♥ HOW TO BE A GOOD WIFE

- When he comes home, have dinner ready on time.

- Take 15 minutes to rest so you'll be refreshed when he arrives.

- At the time of arrival, eliminate the noise of the washer, dryer, or vacuum.

- Don't complain if he's late for dinner.

- Have him lean back in a comfortable chair or suggest that he lie down in the bedroom.

- Arrange his pillow and offer to take off his shoes.

- Never complain if he does not take you out to dinner or to other places of entertainment. Instead, try to understand his world of strain and pressure, his need to be home and relax.

Joni's Note

*There's nothing wrong with doing any of this—as long as it's your choice, and **it's reciprocated by your husband when you need a break.** Back in the 1950s, however, most women's only career choice was to be a housewife— and whether or not they were considered a good one depended on their ability to do the kinds of things on this list—like them or not. Today, you've got a universe of choices, girls, so don't settle for less than you want to be.*

*Your
Teen Years.
The Agony
and
the Ecstasy.*

23

So, What Gives An Old Lady Like Me

I'LL ADMIT IT; it's been a while since I was a teenager. All right—quite a long while. But, this does not disqualify me from helping you learn how to live deliberately during this time of your life.

In fact, because of my past, I think I'm particularly qualified. So do many of my teenage daughters' friends who talk to me on a regular basis. I began my own journey to my dreams when I was about your age. Trust me, it wasn't an easy trip, because my life hadn't been exactly perfect up until then.

the Right to Write a Book Like This?

A Sad, Sad Childhood

I was a product of child sexual abuse. My nightmare began when I was just four years old, and lasted for six long years.

It doesn't really matter who did the abusing, because this book is not about finger-pointing: it's about learning to fulfill our dreams and be happy. So, suffice it to say that my abuser was a boy, somewhat older than I, who my family loved and trusted completely. He was in and out of our house—and our lives—throughout my childhood.

That Boy played upon my shyness and insecurities. He knew I was frail in spirit, and he fed upon that. He was a vampire who sucked the life out of me for a long, long time—much too long.

He pretended to love me and shield me from the world. He said he "understood" me. Because he loved, understood, and shielded me, he expected payment in return. It was a nonverbal agreement. I was too young, and too little to know any better. Everyone in my family trusted him, so I did too.

You may wonder why my parents never knew what was going on. People back then didn't think in those terms—they didn't talk to little children about not letting people touch them intimately.

To add to my trauma, I was held back in the second grade. I hated school. I wanted to be home with my mother, playing sick and being loved and nurtured. That Boy wasn't able to bother me then.

Having to return to the same school and the same classroom in order to repeat second grade was horrifying. The things That Boy was doing to me made it hard enough to look anyone in the eye. Then, when I looked into the window of the second grade classroom, I froze. Those kids would never like me: flunking meant I was stupid and That Boy had told me over and over again that I was an ugly duckling. Being ugly and stupid meant I wouldn't have friends.

Unfortunately, there were no friends that school year. I remember absolutely nothing of the second-grade year

I repeated, except the reverberation of cruel young voices calling me "Flunky."

Sexual abuse. Failure. Fear. Only a few treasured moments of happiness with parents and siblings. That was my childhood. Certainly less than ideal. But, I've come to realize that it was hardly unique, and certainly not an excuse for failing to get my act together years later.

You Don't Have To Let Bad Things Ruin Your Life

Everyone has bad things happen to them. Your bad things may be worse than mine. By some people's standards, they may not be as bad. But, no matter where they fall on the scale, if you allow these things to stand between you and your dreams, you lose.

I said before that being a teenager is wonderful. It's also tough. Good things happen, and so do bad things. You've got to deal with situations and decisions you've never had to handle before. You may think your feet are too big, your hair is awful, or your flat chest is ruining your chances for a love life. You may be so pretty that no one looks beyond the outside to see the beautiful you inside, or expects you to have brains too. (Yes, that **can** be a problem. I have many beautiful friends who get tired of being appreciated only for their looks.)

As a teen, you may have to face situations the world sees as more serious: Mom and Dad may be divorced, someone you love may have a problem with drugs or alcohol, or you may be the victim of abuse, as I was.

No matter how heartbreaking, you have to come to terms with what's bad in your life. Then you have to triumph over it. How do you achieve that victory?

By using what you're learning. Trust me, you're learning consistently during your teen years. You're learning that to live the life you want to lead from this day forward, you can also rely on your *muliebrity*—those qualities and powers you naturally possess as a woman. You may be asking yourself, "Am I a woman now?" A woman is an adult female human being. So, let's say you are definitely "in training" if you're under the age of twenty-one. You are growing into womanhood now. Along the way, you are going to discover your own beautiful qualities and the powers that lie beneath them. That's exactly why this point in your life is exciting!

Together, we're going to talk about many of those qualities and powers, and how they can help you on your personal journey to fulfillment.

How I Started My Journey

My own journey to my dreams began when I was little and when the abuse was still going on. At the time, I had no idea I'd started down the path to fulfillment: I simply knew that if I ran fast enough and far enough, That Boy couldn't catch me. Now, I recognize that the first step on that path was movement, exercise, and a sense of control over my own body. In later years, that extended to eating right and practicing good nutrition.

Later, I recognized that people responded positively if I did good things. So, I trained myself to be of service to others. I also realized that if I looked good, people treated me as though I were pretty. So, I learned to dress well, because I wanted that reaction. As I said before, all the time That Boy abused me, he told me I was an ugly duckling, and I believed him. Therefore, I couldn't completely accept compliments as true, although I hungered for them. Thinking that we're ugly or being called ugly seems to hit home for many of us in our school years. And, it doesn't matter which direction it comes from. I guess it's part of our growing up, as getting picked on is too. When we feel ugly and we get picked on we find ourselves fishing for compliments. Try your hardest not to make that a habit, it can be such a turn off.

Developing my externals—movement, service to others, dress—was like forging a beautiful armor around me so no one could really see all the ugliness I thought I had inside. In fact, my armor was so strong that for many years, I pushed all my memories of abuse behind it: out of sight, out of mind.

Those externals did provide me with a kind of happiness. Certainly not the complete happiness I know now, but a happiness I'd never experienced before. There came a time, however, when I was ready to face what had been done to me. As I came to terms with my past, I knew that the power of externals was not enough. I knew that externals might attract people, and might make them like the me they could see. But what was the point, if that wasn't really the me I was inside?

So, for the first time ever, I looked inside myself. Fortunately, the eventual result was a happiness greater than I'd ever imagined. It permitted me to finally fulfill dreams I'd had all my life.

However, I've often wondered how many more years of happiness I could have had if I'd been able to deal with those inner issues earlier in life! Part of that inability was a result of the abuse, but some came from my willingness to simply drift through my teenage years without doing a lot of thinking about my life, my dreams, and my goals. All I could think about when I was young were my big dreams which were going to happen some way, some day—or I was thinking about my immediate desire to have fun.

This Book Can Help You on Your Journey

Don't get me wrong: there's nothing wrong with big dreams or having fun right now. But, big dreams don't just happen, and happiness doesn't last if you don't have a clear idea of who you are and how you regard the important issues of life.

I hope this book helps you do now what I wish I'd done when I was your age: look at issues that bear examination at this point in your life—boys, sex, parents, excuses, discipline, making choices, having courage, and serving others. We're going to look at the impact that perfect strangers and perfect

If there's someone older out there living one of your dreams, pay attention to her. Do a little research and find out what steps she took. Even ask how she got there.

We all love to share our success stories. And, imitation is the highest form of flattery!

friends have on our lives. We'll talk about the importance of prayer and a relationship with God. We'll also examine the externals that kept me going for so long: dress, exercise, nutrition. Those externals are the outer packaging that can make people want to look inside and get to know you better. And, of course, we're going to focus on the qualities you're learning, as well as your *muliebrity*, those qualities you naturally possess and are developing as a female—-as you grow into womanhood.

I pray that in this process you may accomplish the following:

- Examine your values
- Establish your priorities
- Set your standards
- Form your opinions

For each time you do, you will have made an important stopover on the journey to your dreams. You'll also buy yourself more years of happiness in the bargain.

So, What Are Your Dreams?

DREAMS ARE YOUR DESTINATION. Without dreams, you'll wander aimlessly through life without a clear idea of where you're headed or even what road you're traveling. Without dreams, life happens to you. With dreams, you make life happen.

You need big dreams, little dreams, and in-between dreams. Dreams for your teen years, and dreams beyond. You should spend time now thinking about your dreams. Once you know what they are, you need to learn how to live them, and never give them up.

Countless adult women have told me that they wish they'd dreamed bigger, and wish they'd continued to pursue their dreams throughout their lives. Why didn't they? That's worth examining to make sure it doesn't happen to you.

Why Girls Get Off the Track to Their Dreams

One reason those women didn't dream bigger is that they sabotaged their dreams by failing to have confidence in themselves, their abilities, and the "rightness" of their dreams for them.

Let's look at some examples of the self-defeating behavior many females practice all too well, and what I would say to them:

teacher

"I hate school, and, since I'm sixteen, I can quit now. Everybody says I shouldn't quit, but what's the sense of learning a bunch of dumb stuff?"

If you think school is dumb, think about spending the rest of your life in a boring, dead-end job with no opportunity to make more money because you didn't finish high school. Or, think about how it would grind you to have to depend forever on welfare, your boyfriend, husband, or parents: when you depend on people that much, they usually think they have the right to tell you what to do. I know I'm pushing it, but why not go to a cool teacher (every school usually has at least one) and explain how you feel? You might be surprised by how much he or she understands and can help you stick it out until you graduate.

"All my friends want a career outside the home, but I'd like to be a full-time, stay-at-home mom someday. What are people going to think of me?"

Number One: Who cares what they think if that dream is right for you? Number Two: You might be surprised at how many people are downright envious of your decision.

"I've always admired my grandmother. She's a real lady who never uses bad language or says nasty things about other people. I always wanted to be like her, but my friends all like to use the f-word and put people down all the time. I want to fit in, so I've started doing it, too, but I feel funny about it."

You feel funny because you're denying yourself your dream of being like Grandma. Ask yourself which feels better: having these friends, or fulfilling your dream? It takes a bit of courage to stick with your standards, but real friends—the kind worth having—give you room to be yourself.

"I have a chance for an internship in my dream career this summer. But it's in another state, and my boyfriend doesn't want me to be gone that long: he says that I'm being selfish."

It's hard to be apart, but why are you dating a boy who won't give up three months of seeing you if it helps you achieve your dream? Who's being selfish here?

"I've always wanted to work in a beauty salon, but all my friends are going to college, and they make fun of me. Maybe I should go to college, too."

It's good that you're not ruling out the possibility of furthering your education; however, not everyone wants or needs to go to college to pursue a dream. I didn't go to college, for example, nor did lots of other successful people who are very happy in their careers. Don't give up a lifelong goal without a lot of careful thought. And, don't always think that it's either-or: you could graduate from beauty school, get a job in a salon, and then take college classes at night. Finally, try not to be hurt by your friends' comments. They've made the mistake of judging how important someone is by what they do. However, people are valuable because of who they are. Your friends may have the grades to get into college, but their attitude toward your decision sure doesn't make them look smart.

"I'm in my junior year, and I know I have to make some decisions about the future. My parents want me to live at home, go to the community college, and become a nurse, like Mom. My boyfriend wants me to go to the same state college he's going to, which is about two hours away. I'm not sure whom to listen to."

Why not listen to yourself? I'm sure your parents and boyfriend want what's best for you; however, what do you want? Do you want to be a nurse? Do you want to live at home? Does the school your boyfriend wants you to attend offer the courses you need to fulfill your dreams? Take time now to seriously think about your dreams and your goals. Too many women are content to let others make decisions for them because they're scared to make decisions themselves. However, what's scarier in the long run? Facing life on your own, or constantly being told what to do? Don't sacrifice your happiness for the so-called security of "being taken care of." As you consider your big, long-term dreams, you need to look at your attributes, not your negatives, and you need to view them in light of your entire life. Three months away from a boyfriend compared to a good start on a lifelong career? Don't give up your life-long-lasting-love, just take a personal time out with love notes along the way! Having both your true love and your dream career is possible. Viewed this way, the choices you have to make get a lot simpler.

Giving Up Big Dreams for Little Ones

Another characteristic I noticed in women who lived with regret over unfulfilled dreams was that they let the details of life, even lesser dreams, get in the way of their true longings.

Many girls dream of having a boyfriend, for example. But, if you have to sacrifice a bigger dream—like that internship—to keep him, you're headed for the Land of Lifelong Regret. If you want to be popular so badly that you compromise your heartfelt values to fit in by doing drugs, drinking, or having sex—well, I can guarantee that you'll eventually look back and feel diminished, less like the person you once dreamed of being.

The lessons I still carry with me:

Work hard and you can earn money.

With money comes independence.

Independence is fueled by courage.

Courage makes dreams come alive.

Bottom line: There is no better feeling than making something happen because of your own effort and stick-to-it-ive-ness.

There's nothing wrong with dreams for the short term: boyfriends, prom dates, having friends, making the soccer team. But, to ensure your happiness, make certain your short-term dreams are compatible with your lifelong values and your long-term dreams.

Do You Know What Your Dreams Are?

What are your dreams? Don't tell me you don't have them. Every young woman has hopes in life that won't be denied. They drive you. You can try to achieve your dreams, or spend a lifetime regretting the fact that you didn't.

So, I ask you again: what are your dreams? What is it that you want to do? To become? What dreams do you grant yourself? Are they big, or small, secret, but equally worthy dreams you long to pursue?

But, now that I've asked, don't tell me. Tell yourself. Your dreams should be your secret, never to be divulged. As women, we have the strength of mystery, and we should hold on to that incredible asset. Just work quietly towards making your dreams come true, and let the rest of the world marvel at your accomplishments.

Our dreams come in all sizes, shapes and colors: the life and choices they represent are our very own. Always remember that what's good for one person may not be good for another. Your mother's, sister's, boyfriend's, or friend's dreams may not be the same as yours, and rarely is life spent more miserably than when you try to pursue a dream that is not truly yours.

Paradoxically, the most important part of fulfilling dreams may not be the dreams themselves. Instead, what's most important, most lasting, and most fulfilling may be the inner qualities you develop in the process of achieving your dreams. Once you have those inner qualities, no one can take them away from you, and you can build on them throughout your life to do even greater things.

Bottom line, girls, it comes down to having confidence in yourself. And believing, with all your heart and soul, that your dreams can come true.

"The Fall of the Catholic School Girl"

At twelve, I was experiencing all the wonders and horrors of that time in life: wanting to be a grown-up, yet clinging to the familiar comforts of being a little girl. I was consumed by makeup and hair, and wanting cool, hot-looking teenage clothes, yet did not have a body that was filled out enough to wear them. I was getting interested in boys, but had to have my best friend ask them if they liked me.

I was as confused as any other girl at age twelve. But, there was one thing of which I was certain: I did want to look like a girl.

You see, I had been cursed (I thought then, anyhow) with super curly, unruly hair. I didn't know what to do with it! Neither did my mom. So, once a month, like clockwork, she marched me to the beauty shop and had it cut as short as possible—and buzzes weren't in style back then!

I hated my short hair: it didn't move, it didn't shine, and I couldn't lift it off my collar the way all the cool girls did. The worst was that when I'd meet strangers, like salesclerks, they'd always call me "son." "Son, could I help you?" they'd ask, and I just wanted to curl up in a ball and die from embarrassment.

I began to save my money from babysitting to purchase the one thing—the key item, the answer to my prayer, the big solution—that would eliminate my problem forever: a fall.

What the heck is a "fall," you ask?

It's a long, straight, silky, shiny hair piece: like a wig, but it doesn't cover your entire scalp. It's attached at your crown, so you can let your own bangs hang free. A fall is similar to hair extensions, without the permanence or expense.

Anyway, my fall was the most beautiful thing I'd ever seen in my entire twelve years on earth. I first discovered it one Saturday afternoon in a downtown department store, and, from then on, I was focused on just one goal: to earn enough money babysitting to buy that fall. In the meantime, I rode the bus downtown every Saturday to try the fall on and admire my silky, flowing, new beauty. With my fall in place, I was the beautiful, feminine creature I'd always dreamed of being. Nobody was going to mistake me for boy with my fall in place!

At last, the fall was mine. When I took it home, my family was appropriately admiring of my new look. In fact, my parents even gave me permission to wear it to school. Back then, I attended a Catholic school, complete with the itchy, wool, plaid uniforms we all wore in the 1960s, and nuns in long, black habits with huge blacked-beaded rosaries hanging at their sides. It was a scene out of "Sister Act," minus the laughs.

If I'd been thinking straight, I would have realized that going from a one-inch, curly buzz cut to long flowing locks would be a bit much for good old St. Whoozit's to handle. But, I was completely wrapped up in how I'd reached my goal, made my dream come true, and finally become the ravishing, feminine creature I always wanted to be. Fortunately, for a while, I was able to revel in my new-found beauty: my friends "oohed" and "aahed" on the bus and in the halls as we went to class. I loved being the center of attention, of being seen as cool and pretty at last.

Sister Laverne, however, didn't think I was cool or pretty. A few seconds after I seated myself at my desk, she ripped my fall—my beautiful, silky, gorgeous hair—from my head, and called me a slut!

I was stunned. Then I burst into tears, started hitting Sister Laverne, and screamed, "I am not a slut! I am not a slut! My mother gave me permission to wear this to school."

The embarrassment of that moment! In a few seconds, Sister Laverne reduced me—an independent, driven, self-motivated, hard-working girl—to the size of a pea in front of my peers. And, I reacted by doing the unthinkable: I actually punched a nun!

But, you know what? While Sister Laverne had her momentary victory, I won the war. Despite her actions, she could not take away the lessons I'd learned through the entire experience. She didn't erase my new-found confidence in my potential to be beautiful. Most importantly, she could not take away the self-esteem I gained through making my dream a reality.

No one can do that to you—unless you let them. Remember that as we travel through this book, exploring together how you can pursue the dreams and values that will contribute to the person you want to be—from this day forward.

In case you are wondering what happened to the fall, that long, silky, straight hairpiece was never worn again. The mission was accomplished. Besides, after that kind of embarrassment, you don't take the chance of repeating!

To Achieve Your Dreams, Remember Your ABCs

Avoid negative sources, people, places, things and habits.

Believe in yourself.

Consider things from every angle.

Don't give up and don't give in.

Enjoy life today: yesterday is gone and tomorrow may never come.

Family and friends are hidden treasures: seek them and enjoy their riches.

Give more than you planned to.

Hang on to your dreams.

Ignore those who try to discourage you.

Just do it.

Keep trying, no matter how hard it seems.

Love yourself first and foremost.

Make room somewhere for letting others in.

Never lie, cheat, or steal: always strike a fair deal.

Open your heart and your eyes will see things as they really are.

Practice makes perfect.

Quitters never win and winners never quit.

Read, study, and learn about everything important in your life, and the world.

Stop procrastinating.

Take control of your own destiny.

Understand yourself in order to better understand others.

Visualize it with a picture perfect mind.

Want it more than anything.

Xcellerate your efforts.

You are unique of all God's creations: nothing can replace you.

Zero in on your target and go for it.

— Anonymous

The next page is for you to list your dreams, record your thoughts, write an example, or do anything you wish. You can even send it to Joni (I love to get mail!).

Joni Arredia
c/o Perc Publishing
P.O. Box 351030
Toledo, Ohio 43635

PHOTO BY KAREN BOWERS

SEX, BOYS & YOU

DATING BOYS. Wow! You finally hit thirteen, you're a teenager, and dating is all you can think of.

I've got a little secret for you: until the day you get married, dating and finding Mr. Right will probably be at the top of your priority list. Along the way, you might make some stinky choices or some untimely choices. But, you will make choices.

Choices are what dating is all about. Dating is the first time you really make your own choices about the people in your life, and believe me, they're not always going to be great choices—but that's okay, as long as you know enough to let go of the bad choices.

Smart dating is about finding out, through the choices you make, what you like and don't like in boys. (More on the subject of *like* later.) If you're really smart, dating also involves figuring out how guys fit into your life and your dreams. Do yourself a favor and begin to consider this at an early age.

If You Have Positive Male Examples

Some of you are growing up with what I call "positive" males in the house: a dad, brother, or even grandfather who demonstrates what is best about men. Females who grow up in those homes are so blessed: you can learn early on about good relationships between men and women. As you enter your teen years, you have a better chance of distinguishing between boys who are worthy of your attention and boys who aren't.

If You Don't Have Positive Male Examples

But, what if you grow up in a house where there are no males? That happens a lot these days. And, what if you are growing up in two homes: one with a strong, positive man and the other with a real creep who victimizes you? Or, what if you're surrounded by nothing but selfish creeps in both? What if Mom and Dad are still together, but they do nothing but yell and scream, and you feel like a casualty of war?

Then what the heck are you supposed to think? Do you love men or do you hate them? Do you trust them or not? Do you worry that part of being female is being victimized, since you've seen it happen to the women around you? Can you ever be safe? Can you have a normal, loving relationship?

It's mass confusion, I know. And I am sorry, so terribly sorry. No young person should have to live with this, but so many of you do.

Don't Blame Yourself

If you're in a house where the adults are making mistakes, never think it's your fault. Your Mom or Dad didn't leave because of anything you did. The fact that there's hitting going on, if your dad hits your mom or someone is hitting you, is not your fault. Don't ever believe that or let someone else try to make you believe it. The adults have screwed up here, not you.

Your Past Affects the Way You'll Relate to Guys in the Future

If you grow up in a home without a healthy mom-dad relationship, or if your parents are divorced and your dad never bothers to come see you, you'll probably feel like there is a big hole where your heart should be. If that's the case, be aware that you may be overeager to please any guy who pays attention to you—even if he's a total jerk. If you know this ahead of time, you can be on your guard. Although there are a lot of great guys out there, there are also enough bozos to populate a good-sized planet!

While you may not be able to do anything about the way men in your house act now, you can do a lot of thinking at this stage in your life that can ensure your future relationships with guys are better. Even those of you with positive males in your lives should do some thinking now.

I have a friend who was raised in a positive male home who ended up marrying an abusive man. She once told me that it never occurred to her that a man might hit her when he got angry because she'd assumed that all men were like her father. She also bought into the fall-in-love-and-live-happily-ever-after fairy tale. So, when her "prince" arrived, she was swept away by emotion and hormones, and didn't take a look at his character. The clues were there, but she refused to look at them.

Sort this guy stuff out now, gals, while you're young and resilient. Work it out when you're just starting to think about boyfriends.

If you've been raised around positive males, think about what's so good about those "good guys" and don't settle for less in your own relationships. Be on your guard: keep your ears and eyes open. Remember that not everyone out there is like Good Old Dad or Grandpa.

If you've been abused, or have seen your mom abused by a man, tell yourself that life does not have to be this way, and that not all men are creeps. However, also be aware that because you've been raised around creeps, strange as it may seem, you may subconsciously think that is what's normal. In other words, if you aren't careful, you too may end up with a creep. It's no accident that lots of girls raised in abusive homes end up being married to abusive men. Even though you hate abuse, when you're raised around it, it seems normal. Keep reminding yourself that it's not, and that you deserve more, much more.

Think About the Role You Want Guys to Play in Your Life—Now!

Don't just let men—or I guess we should say *boys*—happen. I've known women who had their entire lives planned, dreams firmly in place, who never gave a single thought to how guys fit in. Then, when guys came along, those dreams went out the window, and a lifetime of hard work and heartfelt values with them. In fact, I consider boys—delicious as they are—to be the Number One Threat to a girl's dream if she doesn't decide early on where boys, and eventually men, are going to fit into her life.

Boys **can** occupy a wonderful place in your life, and becoming interested in boys is a natural part of becoming a woman. But, if you want the best of relationships with boys *and* you also want your dreams, it's important that you give some thought to where boys fall into the scheme of things. Generally speaking, women can be pretty naïve about men.

I know lots of women will get upset with me for saying that, but I believe it with all my heart. I've seen women postpone and even abandon their dreams for men. This doesn't mean that always turns out bad. In fact, sometimes a man turns out better than the dream. On the other hand, I've also seen women go out with guys who weren't fit to tie their shoes. I've seen lots of women rush into intimacy with men in an attempt to take a shortcut to love. And, I've also seen women run roughshod over guys without any regard for their feelings.

We may have come a long way, Baby, but many of us still make the same dumb choices when it comes to men that our great-great-grandmothers did. We may be smarter about

QUIETLY SIZE UP that guy you think you want as a boyfriend. Listen to how he speaks to and treats other girls and women: his mother, sister, teacher, your girlfriends. Make no excuses for him if his behavior is bad! Trust your instinct. Then ask yourself, "Is that how *I* want to be treated?"

You always choose first. You pick whom you want to spend time with. Nobody can be a better friend than you. Remember that you are the only person you spend every moment of your life with!

some things today, but the man-women thing is not necessarily one of them.

Let's talk about some of those dumb things women do.

Sacrificing All For Love

I know of a woman, now in her forties, who had a lifelong dream of becoming a doctor. As you may know, becoming a doctor isn't easy: you've got to have top grades, and good recommendations to get into medical school.

But, Kate worked hard from kindergarten on: straight A's, Honor roll, National Honor Society, scholarships to college— she was well on her way to becoming Dr. Kate. Her college professors were impressed. In fact, one called in some favors to help her get into medical school. Things were looking good.

But, something happened along the way: Kate fell in love. That's not necessarily bad. But, Kate fell in love with a man who was threatened by the thought of her becoming a doctor. His job wasn't as prestigious as hers would someday be.

So, Kate quit medical school, and is now working a job her then-boyfriend-now-husband can live with.

Romantic? No.

Stupid? Yes.

But, the most important questions are: Why did it happen? And, how can you make sure it doesn't happen to you?

Kate was smart academically, but she felt a bit inferior socially. Her good grades put off a lot of boys, and she didn't date a lot during high school. Straight A's didn't provide

much comfort on Friday night when everyone—yeah, right—had a date and she was sitting home. So when old macho What's-His-Face started paying attention to her, she fell all over herself doing whatever it took to please him so he'd stick with her. Kate even gave up a dream she'd worked for as long as she could remember.

Kate abandoned her goal because she was ruled by her insecurities, and she'd never given much thought to how guys should fit into her life. She didn't listen to Mr. Macho's demands and think, "Hey, I've had this dream my whole life and I'd make a good doctor, and if you can't handle that, that's your problem." Instead, Kate thought, "Oh, I finally have a boyfriend, and he wants to marry me, and if I want to keep him I need to do what he wants."

Bogus. Absolutely bogus.

Never, never, never give up who you are or the important things in your life for a guy. And, never ever act dumb to get a guy! Brains are beautiful. This doesn't mean you can't change your mind about a dream—but, make sure when you do change your mind that you're thinking clearly and that it's *your* decision based on your strengths, not your insecurities. Remember this always: Any guy worth having will accept you the way you are, and respect your dreams; any guy who doesn't is selfish.

Case closed.

Blinded by Love, Sex, Whatever

I have a friend who is beautiful, brilliant, talented, and successful. But, she ended up in a horrible marriage with a guy she had to support. She'd work a 10-hour day, come home, and he'd take off for the evening, leaving her to deal with two small kids and a house he hadn't bothered to take care of all day. Eventually, they got divorced, but not before he'd become violent and thoroughly broken her heart.

How did my friend end up with such a loser?

Some of it may have been insecurities, like Kate's. But, a lot of it was the fact that this guy was about the sexiest thing you'd ever hope to meet when he decided to turn on the charm. I remember being with her one day and running into him accidentally. When their eyes met, the temperature rose a good twenty degrees and there was enough sexual electricity to light up New York City.

My friend was blind to her guy's many bad qualities—more than I can count—because of her emotions. Part of that is the result of fairy tales we read and TV shows and movies we watched when we were little. We think that if we feel the emotions of love—those are your hormones in overtime, girls—then we, too, will live happily ever after.

Don't get me wrong: sex is a pretty terrific invention, and it is part of a good relationship when the time is right and you're mature enough to handle it. But, it's not the only thing a relationship should have going for it. If a relationship is to be successful—no matter what age you are—you need to spend time talking, going places, being with other people, and sharing life in general. If all you've got going for you in a relationship is that he's a great kisser, you're headed down the Highway to Heartbreak. (We'll talk lots more about sex later.)

Buying the Fairy Tales of Books, TV and Movies

Earlier, I mentioned a friend who was raised around good men, but ended up in an abusive relationship. Part of her problem was that it never occurred to her that men could be abusive. (Domestic violence wasn't talked about then the way it is now.)

But, the biggest part of her problem was that she believed in fairy tales. Several of them, in fact.

The first fairy tale she bought was that she "needed" a man and that somehow she wasn't complete without one.

The second, that she'd live happily ever after.

The third, that her prince would have to be tall, dark, and handsome, with an air of mystery.

The fourth, that he would cherish and protect her forever.

Time for a little myth exploding here.

The first fairy tale is absolutely false, no matter what the circumstances. A woman does not need a man to make her complete. The best relationships happen when two complete people come together and create something even better between them. Besides, why would you want to walk around as half a person, waiting for the other half to show up before you could get on with life?

Build your lives, girls, and boys will fall into place. I know that sounds too easy, but it's the truth. Would you seriously want to be hooked up with a guy who was so insecure that he only wanted half a woman?

Fairy Tales 2 and 4 can come true, but only if you pick the right guy. My friend thought somehow it would all work out automatically. She didn't realize that a lot of it had to do with the character qualities of the guy she married. She didn't pick up on clues: he didn't treat his mother very well, and he said nasty things about most women while they were dating. Except my friend, of course. He waited to start in on her until after the wedding ceremony. Then, when verbal abuse wasn't enough, he started hitting her, then raping her.

Let me tell you something right now, girls, and if I sound like Aunt Joni on her high horse, forgive me. But, this is so important.

Never let yourself be abused. If a boy hits you, slaps you, shoves you, or even tickles you long after you've begged him to stop—ditch him. Violent guys don't get better without serious counseling. Men who really love don't hurt. They don't hurt physically, and they don't hurt sexually. If a guy forces you to do something you don't want to do sexually, get out of the relationship—now. If he's always putting you down verbally, especially in front of others, run fast and far.

Don't think it's an accident, or that he'll change. There are women who go to the emergency room every day who thought that. Don't think it can't happen to you. Did you know that more than half of all married women are victims of violence at some time during the life of their marriage? And, don't be so stupid—sorry, but there's no other word—to think that his getting violent is a sign that he's macho, in charge, or really masculine. Real men don't abuse women: they protect them, even from their own anger.

Lecture over. Time to shatter Myth 3.

Someday My Prince Will Come

I told you that my friend believed that her prince would be tall, dark, and handsome, with an air of mystery.

Well, he was. But, that gorgeous exterior covered a pretty ugly inside. And, that air of mystery he carried around was really anger and moodiness. Once they were married, he let it all hang out and directed most of it at her.

Don't get me wrong. Not all handsome guys with an air of mystery are secretly evil. There are a lot of great-looking guys who are good through-and-through. But, never make the mistake of judging what's on the inside by the attractive outer packaging.

Take time to hang with guys who are yummy! You know, the kind of guys who are funny, real, sincere, just fun to be with. I've got to tell you, at your age, these guys can be very nerdy and geeky. Not awful, just not the coolest.

I'm going to make a strong pitch for geeky people here. I was a geek. So was my husband. There are famous former geeks, like Steven Spielberg and Bill Gates. The vast majority of geeks grow out of it and end up being sensational people, living exactly the lives they dreamed of. What you are labeled in high school won't stick unless you let it!

Walking All Over Nice Guys

So far I've been talking about friends of mine who made mistakes with guys. On this subject, I don't even need to go that far to find an example. I see her in the mirror every morning.

Because I had been sexually abused as a child, when it came time to date as a teen, it was scary. When I did date, I kept the relationship on the friendship level.

Guys never knew how hard it was for me to be around them in a real-date situation. I was a nervous wreck when a date walked me to my door, because that could mean a kiss—a kiss I was not ready to give.

It was essential to me that I be in control—not a good kind of control, as in knowing what I was doing and how guys fit into my dreams. Instead, I created bad, selfish, nasty control that didn't care who got damaged in the process. I discovered that the less I wanted from a boy, the more he wanted me. I was acting more the way we think guys do: "Hey, I had a good time and you're a lot of fun, but don't call me. I'll call you." That was my way of controlling the relationship, and I reveled in it.

You know what happened because of my attitude? I hurt a lot of great guys, and ruined our chances to really get to know each other.

Women do need to learn how to fit guys in their lives so that they don't let guys pull them off the track to their dreams. However, that doesn't mean you should resort to the kind of dominating, cruel, I-don't-need-you approach I had with boys. I'd been hurt, and I was going to do some hurting for a change; I had been controlled, so now I'd do the controlling.

My attitude toward guys cheated me and used them. But, it did teach me something eventually.

Whenever one partner in a relationship is always dominating, always getting his or her way, always the one around whom all activities and concerns are centered, the relationship is unhealthy. You shouldn't be running roughshod over your guy, and he shouldn't be running roughshod over you. When one person so thoroughly dominates another, it means he doesn't respect her, and it is impossible to truly love someone you do not respect.

Have you ever heard the old Nancy Sinatra song from the Sixties? She used to wear a very short miniskirt and knee-high white patent leather boots when she sang it on television. What she sang about was what I did with guys every chance I got:

> *These boots are made for walking,*
> *And that's just what they'll do.*
> *One of these days these boots*
> *Are gonna walk all over you.*

It wasn't that great a song, and believe me, it's one lousy way to deal with a guy if you want a relationship that brings out the best in both of you.

Rushing Things

Have you ever heard adults say they wished they'd gotten married earlier?

Probably not.

Because most people, especially those who married young, realize that there was no hurry. They just didn't realize it at the time.

At your age, it seems that most of what you do is look forward to growing up. At your age, you're *thirteen-and-a-half* or *almost seventeen.* (At my age, you rarely hear anyone saying that she's *forty-five-and-a-half* or *going on fifty.*) There's a whole world ahead of you, and you can't wait to get at it.

That's good. But, be careful that in your haste to experience life, you don't rush things, especially when it comes to boys. Which, of course, leads to the subject of sex.

You need to know the facts about sex. Remember: knowledge is power, and without an accurate knowledge of what happens, you can end up in a situation you don't want.

I'm going to assume that, at your age, you probably know the basics of sex and how it happens. If you don't, go to your mom, dad, grandma, teacher, or favorite aunt and ask. You're probably going to talk to your friends about sex, but do not rely on them for facts. Friends telling friends about sex is the reason girls come to think that you can get pregnant by kissing (you can't), or that you can't get pregnant during your period or the first time you have sex (you can).

Now let's talk about some of the facts of sex beyond the actual mechanics of intercourse.

Fact #1: Boys and girls are different.

"So, tell me something I don't know," you're thinking. But this is especially true when it comes to sex.

Boys tend to be able to enjoy sex for sex's sake. They can have sex with someone and not get emotionally involved. Girls, on the other hand, tend to attach a lot of emotional significance to sex.

Now, there are people who will disagree with what I've said. I'll admit that there are women who enjoy the act of intercourse just because it feels good. And men usually get

Have you ever heard anyone say, "We're such good friends that I don't want to ruin it with sex?" It happens most of the time: the minute you have sex, you break up. The challenge, the chase has ended. The playful, innocent friendship you started out with just became too serious. Not only did you give away your most sacred possession—yourself—you also lost a friend. Is it worth it?

increased emotional satisfaction out of sex when they're in love with their partner.

However, there are real differences in the way the men and women view sex, and you need to understand them.

Fact #2: Hormones are powerful.

Is there a food you absolutely cannot resist, no matter how hard you try?

My weakness is chocolate-covered peanuts, also known as Goobers.

If there are Goobers in my house, they call my name: "Joni, Joni, come devour us."

If I'm at a party and there's a candy dish full of Goobers, I return again and again until it's empty.

One whiff of a box of Goobers and I'm a goner. I can tell myself I'm just going to eat just one—and the next thing I know I'm sitting with an empty box in front of me.

Passion for Goobers overcomes me!

That's how your hormones (the body chemicals that fuel your emotions and sex drive) can be. One minute you're kissing and he's touching you and the next thing you know, you're going farther than you ever intended to.

Which is why you've got to do with sex what I do with chocolate-covered peanuts. I stay away from situations that get me in trouble with Goobers. That doesn't mean I never eat them, any more than you should never kiss or make-out with a boy once you've been dating a while. But I don't put myself in situations where I'm absolutely alone with a large, economy-size box of Goobers, either.

Remember, when it comes to boys and sex, you have every right to be in control, not the bad kind of nasty control I was so good at, but the God-given right to say what happens to your body and your life. You have the right to use your muliebrity—womanly powers and qualities—to set limits, and avoid situations that might lead to more than you're ready for. (To make sure the "Goobers" aren't within reach, so to speak.) You owe that to yourself, and it's a rare guy who will set those limits for you. Don't look at this and think it's unfair: focus on the fact that it puts you in control—the good kind.

When you're getting physical, remember that once a guy is really turned on, it's darn near impossible for him to stop. Don't get me wrong: he's as responsible as you are for what happens between you, and if he gets so worked up that he forces you to do something you don't want to, he is **wrong, wrong, wrong**—maybe even prosecutable. If that happens, don't ever buy the argument that you were "asking for it"— no matter who says so. Go to someone you can trust and who will listen!

However, do yourselves both a favor and exercise the control that is your right. Also keep in mind that while some guys will respect a last-minute "no," not all of them are gentlemen. If you let some guys go too far they're going to do whatever it takes to have sex. Think about all those stories and movies on TV about date rape. It does happen, and while he's the one who's wrong, *you're* the one who's been raped and has to pick up the pieces.

Sex, Boys
& You

The Guy Game

Fit boys into your life without giving up your dreams—and you win!

START HERE: Your dreams are in place and the whole world is ahead of you!

There's a guy named Bob in your math class you think is cute. Move ahead one space.

You ask your girlfriend to ask Bob if he likes you. He does. Move ahead one space.

You finally talk to Bob between classes. He asks you out. Move ahead one space.

Bob hasn't made any plans for your date: he just wants to make-out.

You don't want to—and you tell him so politely. Move ahead three big spaces.

You don't want to—but you do anyway. Move back three big spaces.

You decide to ditch Bob because you realize he's selfish. Move ahead one space.

Tom, the Captain of the football team, asks you to double date with his best buddy and his girlfriend. Move ahead one space.

Tom talks about himself all evening and puts you down in front of his friends.

If you decide to put up with the abuse, take a detour on the Path to Nowhere.

Ditch Tom and move ahead one space.

You start talking to Zack, the guy who sits next to you in computer class. He's a little geeky-looking, but the more you talk, the more you like him. Move ahead one space.

Zack asks you to the Homecoming Dance.

If you accept him, move ahead one space.

If you turn him down because you're worried about what your friends will think, move back two spaces.

You have a wonderful time at the Homecoming Dance. Some of your friends even tell you they think Zack is kind of cute—in a nerdy sort of way. Move ahead one space.

You tell Zack about your dream of becoming a teacher. He thinks it's great. He tells you about his dream of becoming an electrician. You think it's great. Move ahead one space.

The more you date, the more you like Zack. He wants to have sex, but you're not ready, and you tell him so.

If Zack respects this, move ahead one space.

If Zack is upset and you give in and have sex anyway, move back a whole lot of spaces.

Zack takes you home to meet his parents. He's nice to his mother. Move ahead one space.

You date Zack throughout high school. He's going to the local technical college when he graduates. You want to go to an out-of-state college.

If you change your plans to be with Zack, move back—and plan to keep moving back.

If you both go ahead with your plans, move ahead one space.

You graduate from college and start teaching. Zack has a good job now. You've both fulfilled your dreams and respected each other in the process—so, no matter how your relationship eventually turns out, you're both winners.

Finally, never, never, never be coy and say *no* when you really mean *yes*. That's not fair to your guy. *No* should mean *no,* and both of you should respect that.

Fact #3: Sex is fun, but some of its potential consequences aren't.

I want to establish something here: sex is fun.

I know that anytime an adult starts talking about sex with someone younger, the young person thinks, "What do they know about it? They're too old. They couldn't possibly understand."

But I do understand. I understand that it feels good, and it's a lot of fun, and it's what you naturally want to do when you're attracted to someone, especially after you've gotten close emotionally. Been there, done that.

That said, some of you may wonder why I talk about waiting. "Why should I wait to have sex?" you think. "Everyone else is having it. Why should I miss out on all the fun?"

I respect the fact that this is your decision to make. I just want to pass along some information that may help you as you make decisions about sex.

Whether or not you have sex—and when you have it—should be a conscious decision made at some time other than when you're making-out and things are getting hot and heavy. It's an important decision, and you shouldn't make it when hormones are scrambling your brain waves.

2 **Not "everyone" is having sex.**

I feel sorry for young people today, because television, movies, and music make it seem like "everyone" is doing "it." Watch too much TV and you'd think everyone in America is walking around in a hormone-induced trance, spending every waking moment getting it on. They're not. Trust me. They're too busy getting on with the business of living to spend 24/7 between the sheets.

Our entertainment industry also makes it look like "everyone" jumps into bed immediately with a guy they've just met. In other words, we're told that's normal—even expected— behavior. But that's not the way it is for lots and lots of people. In this day and age of AIDS, why would anyone with two brain cells to rub together hop into bed with someone they just met?

3 Sex is not a shortcut to love. If you have sex so that a guy will love you, you're in for a big disappointment. Women make this mistake all the time. Then, when the guy doesn't like them anymore than he did before sex, they feel empty and used.

4 **The fun of sex lasts for minutes; the consequences of sex can last a lifetime. First, there are sexually-transmitted diseases, some of which, like herpes, never go away. Even those that can be eventually cured, like syphilis, gonorrhea, and chlamydia, may have long-term complications.**

Then, there's AIDS. Get AIDS, and you could die: it's as simple as that. While there are ways to reduce the risk of AIDS, such as condoms, the only absolutely sure way is to practice abstinence (not having sex) until you make a commitment to a life partner who has either also practiced abstinence, or is willing to be tested for AIDS *before* you have intercourse.

Sex is great, but it is not worth dying for.

Second, have sex and you can get pregnant.

In the USA there are
10,000
unplanned pregnancies that happen everyday.

7,000 **of the 10,000 unplanned pregnancies in the USA are**
girls ages 15-24.
Sure, there's birth control, but even the most reliable methods are not foolproof.

Every 20-26 seconds an adolescent gets pregnant.

So, are you ready to have a baby at age eleven or twelve, or even seventeen or eighteen? Can you still pursue your dream while you work to support your baby?

How are you going to feel when your friends want to hang at the mall and you've got to stay home and take care of your baby? You can still go to college if you want, but you'll miss out on all the fun of dorm living and sorority life. There aren't too many mommies who are cheerleaders or homecoming queens, either. If that's not your scene, just substitute what is and then ask yourself whether or not it would be as easy—or even possible—to do it with a baby in your arms.

What about putting your baby up for adoption? Or having an abortion? There are 1,100 teenage abortions that we know of happening everyday. These are serious decisions that you need to think about carefully. Ask yourself if you might feel differently about your decision in ten years than you do now. Do not let anyone coerce you into a decision you're not comfortable with. When that happens, you're a victim of someone else's opinion. Instead, exercise your muliebrity and make the decision that's right for you. Hard as it may be to take control of your life and make a stand, it will be harder in the long run to live with a decision that you don't agree with deep down inside.

5 *You can only have sex for the first time once. Pretty obvious, but think about it. The first time you have sex, you owe it to yourself to be with someone you love. You want it to be incredible. You want to feel cherished, beautiful, protected, cuddled, cared for. You want to experience the joy of waking up with that person the next morning and talking about everything and anything. That's how it ought to be.*

So, tell me how that's going to happen in the backseat of your current crush's car.

You know, I believe that when women think about sex the way they want it to be, it's like couples ice skating. Romantic music swelling, and her costume is floating in the breeze, and he looks studly in tight pants and his shoulders are about eight feet wide. He lifts her and holds her and looks at her tenderly and then there are some spectacularly sexy jumps and lifts. He's so strong and masculine; she's so fragile and feminine. All the moves they make are beautiful and totally in sync and the ice fairly melts from the sexual heat being generated.

Sex *can* happen that way. But the chance of it happening like that when you're cramped in a car, or you're in the basement rec room and his parents are due home any minute? Nada. Zip. Zilch. No way, José.

Sex like that isn't couples ice skating: it's ice hockey. You deserve so much more than that, girls. You should have romance, love, cherishing, and the freedom to simply relax and enjoy it.

When the time is right, you can have all that and more. Don't cheat yourself out of it by indulging in secret sex on the run. The fact that sex is "forbidden" and that you have to sneak around to have it can make it seem pretty attractive, sort of like scarfing down ice cream when no one's looking. But, the conditions under which you have to sneak it are usually far from romantic. And, you deserve better!

As I RE-READ what I've written so far in this chapter, I realized that you may think all my friends—and me—who made big mistakes with men are real losers.

But we're not.

We're actually pretty cool. We've got our acts together. We understand our muliebrity and use it positively to enrich our lives and those of others.

You see, when it comes to men, few women are exempt from making mistakes.

You know who those few are? They're the ones who spent time early in their lives figuring out how guys fit into the scheme of things. They're the ones who are dedicated to achieving their dreams. They date, but they're not about to abandon what they want just because some selfish, fifteen-year-old wannabe stud with terminal acne tells them to.

These few know what they want and have confidence in the rightness of their dreams for them. Instead of rushing things with guys, sacrificing all for love, and buying fairy tales or wearing those "boots made for walking," these wise young women use their teen years to date lots of guys, learn what they like and don't like in a guy, and discover the ins and outs of positive relationships.

Notice that I said "like," not love. I have a little story to share with you. Keep in mind that you're a long way off from this scene, but it's good to understand it now. It may help you with your choices later.

A mutual acquaintance introduced us.

I was twenty, and fell in love with him.

He was thirty-three, and fell in <u>like</u> with me.

When I first met him, this confirmed bachelor, I couldn't stand him. He was cocky and full of himself. And, I was not interested in dating at all, let alone him. I was sick of guys and their lines.

But he sensed that, and he cut me no slack. And, I certainly wasn't going to cut him any with my attitude.

So, we both played hard to get during our first time together that our friend arranged for us.

We were challenging each other, yet we were both intrigued.

We were both acting the same way, boy and girl version. It was funny actually, because we'd each met our match!

So, we started seeing each other. I felt I had known him my whole life.

That first real date, we spent all day shopping, playing at the park and having dinner: a long first date, and I was exhausted. So, we went back to his apartment to watch TV.

I fell asleep on the couch, only to wake up and find that I had drooled on his shoulder. And, he liked me anyway.

I think that was precisely when I fell in love.

The three words we girls want to hear most when we're dating is "I love you." But I never heard those words from him in the two-and-a-half years we dated.

I'd hear, "I like you so much," but never "I love you."

I couldn't stand it.

I mean, after several months of spending day after day together and having a ball, how could he not know he loved me? It drove me crazy!

So, we broke up a couple of times and dated others—and then found ourselves back in each others' arms.

I learned a lot during those times apart from him. I found that other guys didn't like me, just for me, like he did. I began to get the picture: how easy it it was for other guys to say "I love you." But, how could they love me when they didn't even know me, let alone know me well enough to know if they liked me?

Did other guys say those words because they thought that was what I wanted to hear? Or because they might get to first base—or beyond—if they uttered them?

I came to realize that those three words we are all dying to hear from a guy—I love you—are too often just a line of bull.

But, my lovely guy's "I like you"—now there was a meaningful phrase: it said "I enjoy spending time with you, anytime, anywhere." **That** is something to get excited about. How many people do you know who feel that wonderful way about each other?

After two-and-a-half years, my great guy asked me to marry him—with those words I had so longed to hear: "I love you, Joni."

And you know what?

As beautiful as those words sounded when he said them, it's "I like you" that has kept us together all these years, twenty to be exact.

When I finally asked him why he never said "I love you" when we were dating, his answer was so wise:

"Joni, you can love anyone. It's much harder to like someone."

When we started this chapter, we talked about dating as making choices. Think hard as you make these choices, girls. Make good ones, and you won't have to waste time digging yourself out of bad ones, like my friends and I did.

Whom you choose to be with says a lot about who you are and how you think about yourself. Never, never sell yourself short by choosing to be with someone who's less than the wonderful guy you deserve. Never give up your dreams for a guy. The ones worth having won't ask you to.

Don't let your emotions get in the way of your good sense. If he doesn't really like you, and you don't really like him, it's not love, girls, it's hormones. Acting on hormones alone—

without liking—leaves you empty inside, sort of like eating cotton candy. Looks good, tastes good, and doesn't do a single thing to nourish you or help you grow.

And, growing is what this time in your life—and our trip through this book—is all about.

PHOTO BY KAREN BOWERS

CHANGES, CHOICES, AND THE COURAGE TO SERVE

RIGHT NOW, you're entering—or going through—one of the greatest periods of change in your life, the process of changing from a child to an adult. Whenever you face change, you have choices to make—-even if you decide to do nothing.

Because adolescence is such a tremendous time of change, it's also a time in which you have many choices to make. In fact, a big part of the change taking place is that you're traveling from a point in your life where Mom and Dad made all your choices for you to a point where you'll be making most choices yourself.

The Importance of Making Mistakes

In the process of making choices, you'll make mistakes, fall down, and even get a bit bruised. But, if you make your choices with your values in place, your dreams firmly set in front of you as a guide, you probably won't fall as far or bruise as badly.

I have one thing to say about mistakes: Make them! Show me someone who makes no mistakes, and I'll show you a person who makes no choices. If you make choices, you make mistakes, but that's how you learn. You may be embarrassed, but at least you're moving forward—and never moving forward is eventually a whole lot more embarrassing!

 Remember the story, "The Fall of a Catholic School Girl"?

Making Better Choices

The prospect of making choices should excite you, because you can make so many good ones. You can choose to learn new skills, expand your horizons, and make new friends. If you have parents who don't care, you can begin to make choices in life that will ensure that someday you will be a good parent. If you've been treated badly, you can choose to never treat others that way.

Don't do what too many women have done in life: don't allow the bad things that have happened to you in the past control you forever. Choose, instead, to move beyond the pain and live the life you want and fulfill your dreams.

Breaking the chain of the miserable events of your past and moving far, far beyond is the sweetest success. Remember, however, that even if you choose to live life differently than you've experienced it in the past, you may find yourself slipping back into old patterns at times. Maybe you realize you're treating someone the sad way you used to be treated.

Or, maybe you realize you're using a tone of voice you swore you'd never use.

That's when you have a choice to make. Choose right then and there to get a grip on yourself and change your behavior. Don't beat yourself up. It's human nature to slip up. On the other hand, don't allow yourself to continue on your backward slide. Choose change instead!

Put Your Intuition to Work

As you make choices, use your intuition, girls. I've heard different women describe intuition in a variety of ways: *the feeling I get in the pit of my stomach,* or *chills all over,* or *my gut reaction,* or, simply, *a sense of what I should do.*

How ever it's defined, intuition tells you what to do, right now, without hesitation. It is not something you can explain logically. It's grasping the feeling, not necessarily the facts, of a situation, and knowing instinctively what you should do. Men may have intuition—I don't really know. Women, however, have it in abundance. Intuition is one of our strongest and most reliable assets.

If you really listen to your intuition as you face choices in life, it will always steer you in the right direction. The only time I get in a bind is when I don't listen.

Quick story. I was on my first day of vacation having lunch at a crowded, loud, lively restaurant on a pier in South Florida. We all ordered the same fish sandwich. The food came and my fish didn't look or feel quite as cooked as theirs. So, I carefully ate around the edges, then stopped. The waitress came over to check on our meals and I nicely explained that my fish was rubbery in the middle. She assured me it was fine. Well, why wouldn't I believe her, she had worked there for years and was delightfully funny. Huge mistake! Later that night I got an awful feeling in the pit of my stomach. The kind of sick feeling when you know you're going to be camped out on the cold tile floor next to the toilet all night. Ugh—food poisoning. I thought I was dying, no kidding! I wouldn't wish it on my worst enemy. The first thought that came to mind when I woke up sick—*why didn't I listen to my intuition!* In a bind? You betcha, in more ways than one. That was one lousy vacation! Trust your intuition always.

It Takes Courage to Make Choices

Sometimes making choices is scary: change always is. That's why accepting change, and making choices to meet its demands, takes a mammoth amount of courage.

What is courage? I think it's the quality of being bold. A sense of fearlessness. Standing tall in the face of rejection, fear, difficulty or danger. Facing adversity head-on. Holding so fast to your dreams and beliefs that nothing can knock you down.

Courage is saying "no" when a cool girl or guy forces you to make a choice about alcohol or drugs. It's refusing to join in when everyone else is verbally abusing the class nerd. It's choosing friends who share your values, even if they're not as popular as the kids who don't. In a society that has elevated self-concern to an art form, one of the greatest acts of

I have a friend whom I admire more than anyone else in the world. This is the motto he lives by:

To try and to fail is to learn, but to fail to try is to suffer the inestimable loss of what might have been.

courage you, as a young woman, can perform is to purposely choose to serve others.

Choosing to Serve Others

The benefits of serving others are endless. Something as simple as bringing a smile to another's lips is an incredible gift of service, and as easy as turning up the corners of our mouth first. But, because we fear rejection, smiling first takes that thing called courage.

What if she doesn't smile back? Well, hang on, because the truth is that she usually doesn't, at least not immediately. Ah, but if we can hang on to that smile and summon up our courage to maintain eye contact for another ten seconds—voila—we will encounter the most beautiful sight, another's smile. And, we will also have—if just for a second—changed our world for the better.

I have been on both sides of this scenario. As a young girl, I found it difficult to smile. So when I was little and someone took time to get me to smile, it felt so good, and the look on that person's face just made it feel better. There we were: two warm beacons of light, illuminating that particular space and time for a single, perfect, shared moment.

After a while, I found that sharing smiles was so simple, yet it made me so happy. No words, no touch, just brilliant smiles that helped heal me. As a result, by the time my childhood had passed, my smile was a permanent fixture on my face.

Let's always remember the beauty, and the power, of a simple smile. When we smile, we make another human being feel important, special, even loved, for a single moment in time. And, in some lives, unfortunately, that single moment may be the only speck of caring that person has experienced in ages.

We also do something for ourselves with that smile. We exercise our courage. We gain freedom from that moment because we're in charge, reaching out first in the face of potential rejection. We suck in a deep breath, step outside of our comfort zone, and *willingly serve.*

In turn, we realize an exhilarating freedom that can become habitual, intoxicating to us, and contagious to others. And that, my darlings, is what it's all about: that's when we start to change the world—and ourselves—for the better.

For me, serving others began on the riverbank near my childhood home where I cared for small, injured animals. Later, in high school, it bloomed fully when I volunteered at the State Hospital in order to earn school credits. The hospital was designed to house people with mental problems.

Once a week, my school friends and I drove onto the grounds, at first seeing the adult house with its tower, its residents screaming and shaking the bars on the windows. That brought tears to my eyes every week: pretty nerve-wracking stuff for a sixteen-year-old—or maybe no matter what your age. It took all the courage I had some weeks! But, I know that we brought light into the lives of the teens we helped there, so it was worth it.

You Can Choose to Change Your World

Serving means noticing a need, then following through and filling it. That takes kindness, strength, generosity, and power: in other words, muliebrity.

As a young woman, you undoubtedly see much in your world that needs to be changed, many areas that cry out for your service. In your heart of hearts, you know when things are not the way they should be, and that circumstances exist that no one should have to live with. You sense there should be a change, even a mutiny—and you know what? You should choose to lead it!

As women, you are the ones who can. Women are survivors, pure and simple. And, over the centuries, while men were busy getting their names in the history books, women were the ones quietly making choices that shaped the day-to-day life that is the very foundation of civilization.

It took courage to make right choices then, and it takes courage to make those choices now. But, in the end, the world is better for your courage and choices, and so are you.

Take a minute to think about the last teeny-weeny, kind choice
you made for another's sake.
How did it make that person feel? How did it make you feel?
If your answer is "really good," keep doing it!

CHAPTER SIX

Lose the Excuses. Find the Discipline.

$$12x + 17 = 45$$
$$12x + 17 - 17 = 45 - 17$$
$$12x = 28$$
$$x = \frac{28}{12} = \frac{14}{6} = \boxed{\frac{7}{3}}$$

EXCUSES. As teenagers, we make a million of them.

We come up with some real doozies, particularly if we think we're going to disappoint a parent or teacher. Making excuses beats being grounded or getting a detention.

We make excuses when we feel insecure about our ability to achieve a goal. Most of the time, it's because we can't figure out how to begin. The task looks monumental and getting started is always tough and, and, and…we end up scared and stop trying before we even start.

It seems better not to do anything than to mess up and make a huge mistake. So, we say we're too stupid or we're not interested, or that it's a lame idea. Along those same lines, we constantly make excuses for our appearance. "Oh, my hair is a mess." "I look terrible today." "I've got all these horrible zits." "I am *so* fat."

We're making excuses to avoid the embarrassment of failing, or to point out our own inadequacies before others have the chance to.

A Sign That You're Not in Control

Remember how we talked earlier about the importance of making mistakes, because that is how we learn? If you never try anything, always making excuses instead, you're going nowhere fast—and telling the world loud and clear that you're a victim instead of a victor.

So, make a deal with yourself: no more excuses! No one wants to hear them anyway.

Making excuses tells others that you don't have control of your life and that you have to blame something or someone other than yourself. By focusing on inadequacies, you're telling others you don't really respect yourself; eventually, you'll start to really believe that you don't measure up.

When you find yourself making excuses, it's time to take the responsibility of working hard to control your life. How are you going to do that? By making a new best friend: DISCIPLINE.

Your Best Friend

Okay. Right now you're thinking to yourself, "I was with her right up until now. But 'discipline is my best friend?' Yeah, right! Discipline is a set of stupid rules adults make up that I have to follow. It means doing what I am told when I am told. Discipline is what my dog needs in order to be properly trained—but I'm not a dog. I don't need that kind of training!"

If you're not sure what discipline is, watch someone who makes things happen. You'll find that they balance their time with things they have to do and things they like to do. Every single time!

I hear what you're saying. But, don't give up on me now! Because, when I say *discipline,* I'm not talking about gritting your teeth and being miserable. By *discipline,* I mean doing what's necessary to get you to your dreams. Let's take a look at that dog analogy for a minute.

Your puppy—let's call her Lucy, a great name for a dog—comes in every morning, jumps on your bed, licks your face all over and wakes you up: "Hey," says Lucy in pet talk, "I've got to go outside for a potty break." A couple of days of this, and you know it's going to happen like clockwork. In fact, you almost look forward to it. She depends on you and loves you unconditionally—heck, you've trained her to do that. Because she loves you unconditionally, you've trained yourself to pull your sleepy, groggy, tired body out of bed and open the door for her.

That takes discipline. But, because you love Lucy so much, it doesn't seem like discipline.

That's the funny thing about discipline. When you like what you're doing, or whom you're doing it with or for, it doesn't seem like discipline. But it is.

You've trained Lucy and yourself to take care of each other: you've formed a good-for-you, lasting habit, and acquired stick-to-it-ive-ness. As a result, Lucy becomes the model pet who goes everywhere with you (your Lassie), and your friends consider you a Pet Owner Extraordinaire. You make it look so easy, and everyone wants a dog just like Lucy. When discipline becomes habit—like taking care of Lucy—it looks so easy to everyone else. Only you know it took patience and endurance and character to make it happen.

Lose the Excuses. Find the Discipline.

Something else happened in this process. When you did what it took to train Lucy, when you had the discipline to follow through—you ended up realizing your dream of owning a terrific pet. And, that made you feel really good.

That's why I say that discipline is your friend. Just like a flesh-and-blood friend, it supports you in your pursuit of your dreams. It wants what's best for you. And, when you get off the track to your dreams, discipline, like a good friend, lets you know. It cuts you no slack, and pushes you to see your dream through to its end. That doesn't always feel good at the moment, but you're going to feel even worse if you don't achieve your dream. Just think how bad you would feel if you didn't have the discipline to train Lucy, and you had to take her to the pound because she thought your Mom's favorite rug was her very own private bathroom.

Why Parents are <u>So</u> into Discipline

"Okay," you say, "I buy your argument. But that doesn't explain the discipline my parents impose on me. That's not getting me anywhere near my dreams. It sure doesn't feel good. And they can't possibly understand my life right now."

I know how you feel. When I was your age, I thought my parents were so ancient that they couldn't have ever been young. I figured their goal in life was to impose a bunch of Old Fogey Values on me so that my life would be just as dull as theirs.

But, then I grew up and became a parent myself. You know what? I finally understood why they were imposing discipline on me. It wasn't that they didn't understand what it was like to be young; it was that they understood all too well.

It's hard to imagine, I know, but your parents were young once, too. They wanted to have a boyfriend or girlfriend. They wanted to fit in and be cool. They had to make choices about smoking, alcohol, drugs, and—disgusting as this may be to think about—even Raging Hormones. Mom and Dad know you need to make mistakes to learn, but they don't want you to make really disastrous mistakes because they know how painful they can be.

That's why, until you get a handle on disciplining yourself, adults who care will impose discipline on you. They're not trying to do something negative (even though it seems like it sometimes). What they're doing for you is providing an outer form of discipline to protect you until you've instilled discipline in yourself.

Let me insert something here: there **are** bad parents who don't care. But most do, even if they don't always express it very well. Try to remember that it's hard to be a parent, especially a single parent. Parents spend so much time simply doing stuff—driving places, shopping, cooking, doing laundry, working—that they're often on the verge of total exhaustion. So, if you're living with the kind of parents who do care, cut them some slack when it comes to discipline. They're trying to help you, and you didn't come with an instruction manual. They're doing their best, but they're not perfect.

Now, if your parents really don't care, or if they care, but they're drunk, stoned, or gone so often that they might as well not care—then you need discipline, too, but you have to impose it on yourself as soon as possible. Why? So that **you** don't end up someday being a parent who doesn't care. Learn what you can from this experience, bad as it may be, and practice the discipline necessary to make something better

Lose the Excuses. Find the Discipline.

of your life than your parents have. Then, when you find a partner in life whom you really like, can marry, and have children with, you can take the best of what you both learned growing up and combine it with the best that you are. In this way, you'll do a better job of parenting.

If you can grasp the importance of discipline now, you'll be way ahead of lots of adults who never learned how important discipline is to achieving their dreams. You may know a grownup like this: he or she just floats through life, and may even talk about what could have been. Other adults do understand discipline's importance—they're the ones who shove it down your throats, because, as we've discussed, they know that in the long run it will help you achieve your dreams and happiness all by yourself. And, there is nothing more satisfying than knowing you achieved a goal on your own.

What Discipline Does for You

Discipline helps focus you. When you're focused, you can decide what you truly want. You have to know what you want before you can go after it. Knowing is always **first.** Then you can decide what's important to do right now, what can wait for later, and what may never be wise to do at all.

Getting your priorities straight each day gives you the strength to perservere and never give up, no matter what anybody else may think or how hard it is to get to your dream. This is discipline: the strength to get through the crap and the stuff you don't like to do, but that has to be done to pave the way to your dreams.

Discipline is what keeps you in chemistry class because you want to be a nurse someday, and nurses have to take chemistry, no matter how much they hate it. It's what makes you practice an instrument faithfully, even on those days you don't feel like it, because you love being in the band more than you hate practicing.

Discipline is also the strength to say "no" to something you may really want to do, but that will put a roadblock in that path. It's what makes you pass up what's obviously bad, like using drugs, because it could derail your dreams. But, sometimes it's passing up something that's perfectly okay— like a party the night before the SATs because you want to be rested for the test.

Sad but true: when there's a need for discipline in your life, it usually means that you've got a hard choice to make, and by choosing one thing, you're giving up another you'd also like to have. It doesn't take a lot of discipline to not eat celery; it may take a lot to not eat Doritos.

That's why you need a good handle on your dreams: it isn't nearly as difficult to pass up hot fudge when your dream is to fit into that little sequined number for the prom. You're practicing discipline by doing less of what doesn't get you to your dream—scarfing hot fudge. You may even wish to practice discipline to do more of what does—exercising sensibly, for example.

Discipline also gives you the strength you need to stick with the hard work it takes to achieve your dream. Sometimes we look at someone who has something we wish we had, and we figure she's luckier or smarter than we are. Our imaginations run wild, usually in the direction of our own insecurities. But, when we get to know the person, we realize that her luck is no better than ours, and we're just as smart.

Lose the Excuses. Find the Discipline.

"Mrs. Ohio"

During those dreadful years of my childhood, I believed myself to be quite the ugly duckling because That Boy told me repeatedly that I was. It took years before I felt beautiful, but, by the ripe old age of thirty-three I guess I was feeling pretty sure of myself, at least on the outside, and I entered the Mrs. Ohio pageant.

Whatever possessed me, I'll never know: I'd never done anything like it before in my life.

But, something inside me pushed me to enter, so I did.

Getting ready for the Mrs. Ohio pageant was quite a task. I had clothes to buy—and you can imagine how perfect they had to be—written evaluations to fill out, and an attitude that had to be honed. It was a busy and nerve-racking couple of months, but I was filled with excitement.

The pageant was being held 250 miles from home, and I had absolutely no idea what I was going to encounter when I got there. In the back of my mind, though, I truly believed that the judges would be looking for an older, mature, interesting woman who was the wiser for being happily married.

As the weekend progressed, I realized that I had been sadly mistaken. They were looking for an older version of Miss America, complete with sequins and bathing suits and women who covered their rears with duct tape so they wouldn't jiggle when they walked. Besides that, most of the contestants had been in pageants for years, and knew all the ropes. (Shoot, I didn't even know how to turn at the end of the runway.) And, on top of that, the atmosphere of female cattiness was enough to suffocate the strongest woman.

So, there I was: four hours from home, alone, and in a situation I no longer wanted to be in.

Did I let that situation control me? Did I quit? Question my own values and try to shape myself into what the judges were looking for? Get depressed because I wasn't pretty enough or had the wrong clothes? Did I let those catty women get to me? Did I feel sorry for myself and make excuses?

Absolutely not!

I took that "lemon" and I made lemonade. I kept my mouth shut and eyes and ears open and learned all I could that weekend. I put on my armor against the cattiness, and used my strength to help protect some of the sweeter, softer women, who, like me, were just winging the whole experience.

It was a real lesson in strength covering insecurity—and it worked.

I think the judges were, in fact, looking for a married floozy. But, I stayed true to myself and my values—which do not include being a married floozy—and I ended up as one of ten finalists. I kept the plaque, not because I'm proud that I was a finalist, but as a reminder that I worked my tail off for it. I even purchased a videotape of the pageant, although it took two years before I had the courage to watch it—alone, in my dark basement, in the middle of the night.

And, do you know what I learned when I did? That I was smart! That when I smile, I dazzle people! Watching that tape was exactly the experience I needed to move forward at that point in my journey, to believe more than ever in myself and the direction I was taking in life. It was the first successful assault on my ugly-duckism and feeling like a seven-year-old flunky who had to repeat second grade.

I mentioned that when I entered Mrs. Ohio, I didn't know exactly why. Life is like that sometimes. We do things, not knowing the reason. We're simply compelled. Then, much later, we understand. We understand that this is intuition!

That is why it is essential that you try, stretch, and follow through—especially in this time of your life specifically designed for you to spread your wings and experience new things. What you'll gain is a greater understanding of yourself and the world around you.

I didn't become Mrs. Ohio like I once hoped. I undertook that journey with the highest expectations, but they were focused in the wrong direction. I learned much more by losing than by winning, and I held onto life's most important crown, self-respect.

And, I would have gained none of that if I'd made excuses. ❧

The Benefits of Hard Work

The truth is, there's usually a tremendous amount of hard work—made possible by discipline—behind whatever it is she has that we wish we did. When you want something and you don't have it, it's almost never because you're not smart enough to achieve it: it's because you haven't worked hard enough.

A little story here. I have always considered myself bright, charming and personable—but not always smart. However, since I wrote my first book, *Muliebrity: Qualities of a Woman,* all of a sudden people consider me brilliant.

That's fascinating to me, because I haven't changed. Sure, I grew and learned a lot as I wrote, but I'm basically the same old Joni. The only difference between Joni pre-book and Joni post-book is that I literally worked my buns off to get that book written. It took every ounce of discipline I had to fulfill that dream. People now think I was capable of writing a book because I'm smart, when the truth is that I wrote a book because I worked hard. Discipline made that possible, just as it can help you achieve your dream.

And, when you accomplish that one big dream, you'll feel so good about yourself and your accomplishments that you'll start all over again and reach for another goal. At that point, you won't even consider making excuses. And, you won't be mad that discipline is tagging along. In fact, you'll probably welcome her, and never bad mouth her again. After all, it's not cool to put down your best friend.

Like the best friend it is, discipline keeps you on track. But, a word of warning here: **discipline is not obsession.** *Let's look at this for a minute.*

*Say your goal is to be thin. Discipline helps you make wise choices from all four food groups, eliminate junk food and exercise sensibly. Discipline **does not** help you limit your calories to fewer than 1200 a day, or only eat an apple all day, or exercise four hours to work off the food you ate, or force yourself to throw up your last meal. That is not discipline; that is obsession, and obsession is not a good thing.*

Discipline recognizes this fact: it knows you need balance in your life, doing a little bit of everything so that you don't go overboard and get carried away and obsess about any one thing. When you lose your balance, you either become so overwhelmed that you want to throw in the towel on everything, or you do so much damage to yourself physically or psychologically that you can no longer function normally. In either case, you give up on your dream and have that awful feeling that gets you nowhere.

Remember: *If you tend to be obsessive, sometimes the most truly disciplined thing you can do is just kick back, relax, and hang out.*

On Becoming A Woman

I ABSOLUTELY LOVE being a woman! And it's my prayer that as you grow into womanhood, you'll love it just as much as I do.

Being a woman—dare I even say *lady*—does not mean losing power or strength. On the contrary, when we develop our muliebrity, our womanly powers, we gain immeasurable amounts of control.

I'm not talking here about the cutesy-pie-oh-you're-such-a-big-strong-guy-and-little-ol'-me-is-just-so-lucky-to-be-your-doormat and/or but-what-I'm-really-doing-is-manipulating-you-like-heck brand of control associated with false femininity. I'm talking about true control that results from the kind of feminine strength and dignity that our country so admired in Jacqueline Kennedy Onassis.

A Perfect Example of a Strong Woman

She was the First Lady of President John F. Kennedy, who was assassinated on November 22, 1963, in Dallas. In the 1037 days she graced the White House, Jackie demonstrated an elegant style the nation adored. And then, during that terrible weekend following her husband's murder, she displayed a silent strength and personal dignity that inspired the world.

Jackie Kennedy Onassis had the ability to do all that because she knew who she was. Her values and goals were firmly in place. As her son, John F. Kennedy Jr., said at the time of her death in 1994, "She did everything in her own way and her own time. That is the way she lived, and the example she gave to the world."

What Makes a Woman Strong

To be the best you can be, to fulfill your potential and achieve your dreams, you have to be mighty comfortable in your own skin, just as Jackie was. You have to have one-hundred-percent ownership of the word *confidence.*

Confidence is not cockiness, nor is it ego gone wild. Confidence is not building yourself up by putting someone else down. True confidence comes from acknowledging your accomplishments, not waiting for someone else to acknowledge them for you.

For most of recorded history, women have been viewed as weaker than men, but don't you buy that for a second, girls. Oh, certainly, we may not have the physical strength most men do, but where it counts—on the inside—we have incredible courage and strength of character.

Consider the women you admire. Make a list of the characteristics they share, and I'll bet the following words show up on it: strong, kind, giving, and powerful. That's what you want to be, too, girls. The good news is that you're well on your way!

Adolescence: Land of Changing Hormones

You're also well on your way to—or are already—experiencing the physical, emotional, and psychological changes that come with being a woman.

Again, as with sex, I'm going to assume you know the basics of what's happening physically, why you're getting curves and bumps where you didn't have them before. If you don't, I urge you to talk to your parents or an adult you trust to get the facts. You can giggle all you want with your friends, but don't rely on them for accurate information.

If something's happening with your body that's never happened before, and you don't understand it, go directly (Do not pass Go. Do not collect $200) to that trusted adult and get the information you need to put your mind at ease.

All those changes that are happening to you right now are largely the result of your body's producing hormones in larger quantities than ever before. Your body is producing more of a hormone called *estrogen*, while boys' bodies at this age are producing more of a hormone called *testosterone*. Not only is estrogen responsible for the physical changes you're experiencing, it's also responsible for the different way you may feel.

You may be moodier than you used to be, and even cry more at certain times. You may find yourself attracted to guys now, when just a few short years ago, they were major league disgusting. You may find that you enjoy kissing and hugging guys when just months ago you would have rather swapped spit with a pig. Given that these changes are solely due to your hormones kicking in, you have to know that these are totally awesome chemicals!

The Hazards of Raging Hormones

We talked about this in the chapter on sex, but I believe it bears repeating: Hormones on a Rampage—the kind you feel when you're getting physical with a guy—can carry you away. To keep from going farther than you want to, avoid situations that lend themselves to getting carried away. Remember the Goobers?

Believe it or not, women through the ages—yes, even Mom and Grandma—had to deal with Raging Hormones. They were as curious about sex, and, I dare say, as horny, as you are sometimes. However, there are some big differences between then and now.

- Today we live in a culture that's very sexual, so you're bombarded with sexual messages every day. The more you hear about it, the more curious you get. It's perfectly natural to be curious: just don't let your curiosity lead you into territory you're not prepared to handle.
- Generally speaking, parents in years past exerted more control over their kids than parents do now. Where as today, teens tend to go more places more often without parental supervision, which means they have more opportunities to experiment with sex.

Sex, Boys
& You:
Be Your
Own Best
Girlfriend

104

• A generation or two ago, society's standard was that girls waited until marriage to have sex. Of course, there were girls who didn't wait, but the standard was there, lending moral support to girls who wanted to save sex for marriage. Today, it's widely believed, but not necessarily true that it's unusual for a girl to remain a virgin until her wedding night. Because of that, a girl can't fall back on the societal standard to justify a "no." She has to have her own standards firmly in place. Thank goodness there is a rising move towards waiting. Why? Take another look at excerpts from Chapter 4, Sex, Boys & You.

Keep in mind, get AIDS, and you could die: it's as simple as that. While there are ways to reduce the risk of AIDS, such as condoms, the only absolutely sure way is to practice abstinence (not having sex) until you make a commitment to a life partner who has either also practiced abstinence, or is willing to be tested for AIDS *before* you have intercourse.

Also, take another good look at these statistics. They will help to gently remind you.

- **In the the United States of America there are 10,000 unplanned pregnancies that happen everyday.**

- **7,000 out of the 10,000 unplanned pregnancies in the USA are girls between the ages of 15-24. Sure, there's birth control, but even the most reliable methods are not foolproof.**

- **Every 20-26 seconds an adolescent gets pregnant.**

Saying "No" Is Always Okay

As you grow into womanhood and start to date, remember that it's always okay for you to say "no" to any part of getting physical with a guy even after you're married. As we've said before, being female does not have to mean being a victim: it's your right to exercise positive control over your physical relationship with a guy.

However, be aware that your date may not be real happy about that "no." And, he may do some pretty fancy talking to get you to go farther than you'd like. To make sure you're prepared for his particular brand of persuasion, let's look at the various arguments of that species known as the Thwarted Horny Male.

1. *"You're a tease."* What a guy means by this is that you let him do something, or you said you'd do something, and then you changed your mind. Or maybe that you touched him in ways that promised more than you're prepared to deliver.

   So ask yourself, "Did I?" If you did, apologize, then make certain you don't do it again. Even if you did tease, that doesn't mean you're obligated to proceed to sexual intercourse.

2. *"You're uptight."* Puh-lease!! I'm sure that this is what the First Caveman said to the First Cavewoman on their First Date when he wanted to make-out and she didn't. He's questioning your ability to be a woman, hoping to get you to have sex to prove you're a real female.

3. *"If you loved me, you'd let me."* Really? Tell him that if he loved you, he'd respect your decision to wait.

4. **"We need to see if we're compatible."** Yeah, sure. You already know you like to kiss and touch. Trust me, you'd also enjoy what follows. And compatible? Well, if he means physically, that's a joke: the Good Lord created men and women with standard parts, give or take a little. If he's talking about general compatibility, then stop making-out and start talking. *That's* how you discover if your relationship is going to work.

5. **"We either do it, or it's over."** So it's over. So what? Why would you want to be hooked up with a loser who has to resort to threats to get sex? This guy doesn't care about you as much as he cares for his needs. And no, despite what he may tell you when he's desperate, he's not going to die if he doesn't have sex.

So, You Want to Be Sexy?

Let's talk about another aspect of growing older—being sexy.

I have never yet met a woman who didn't want to be sexy at some time in her life. But, I'd like to offer you something even better than sexy. I want you to consider, instead, being sensual.

What do I mean?

When you think about being sexy, you probably think of externals such as: hair, clothes, posture, walk, the look in your eyes, your body language. It's what you see on the outside, and it's often the thing you try to imitate as you go through your teens. But, if that's as far as it goes—the outside—it's pretty empty, and it's certainly not a good foundation for a relationship.

When I was a freshman in high school, I was into wearing tight, sexy-looking clothes, and lots of makeup.

The result? One very fast-looking girl. Except I didn't know that's how others saw me. All I knew was that I wasn't getting asked to the homecoming dance like all my friends—and I was devastated.

About that time, my mom was at some school function and overheard some of the other moms talking about this fast-looking girl their sons and daughters had been making snide comments about. That girl was her daughter, Joni.

Mom knew better than to believe that I was fast, but it broke her heart to hear those women talk about me in such an unflattering way. So, that night she came into my room, sat on my bed, and told me what she'd heard. She explained that what I looked like was different than what I really was, that I was sending out the wrong signals.

Mom asked me to lay off the makeup and dress a bit differently, to match the outside with the beauty and kindness she knew were inside me. And it worked!

It took several weeks for the kids to trust the change, but soon a few brave boys started to call. And, after a few honest conversations, I found out that the way I dressed before actually scared them off. Me, who was so scared of them!

It can also get you into some serious trouble. You may just be trying out new things, attempting to be sexy in that skin-tight outfit that barely covers your rump, with actual sex the farthest thing from your mind. But your guy, who is very turned on by visual stimuli—(that's scientific talk for *what he sees*)—may think that if you're giving off sexy signals, you must be as interested in having sex as he is!

How About Being Sensual Instead?

For that reason—and more—I'd like to suggest that rather than concentrate on the outer show of being sexy, you concentrate instead on nurturing your sensuality.

Sensuality is the confidence to reveal your soul, to strut your inner stuff, so to speak, and to have the carriage and attitude to pull it all off. It's what's on the inside, and it's the foundation on which true sexiness (as opposed to purely external sexiness) is based.

External sexiness doesn't last. It's a flash in the pan that breaks the ice—even melts it—but eventually it leaves you standing in the cold if it's all you've got. On the other hand, sensuality and the true sexiness it fuels are steady flames that fire your heart and warm your relationships with others.

Sensuality is a result of great love. Love of people. Love for life. Love of beauty, as each one of us beholds it. Sensuality is awareness. It's appreciation. It's the ability to live life to its fullest.

I think that the major difference between external sexiness and sensuality is your focus. In external sexiness, you're saying, "Look at me. I'm hot. If you're really lucky I'll pay attention to you, and if you're smart, you'll pay attention to me." Sensuality, however, is focused on others, on sharing your zest for living: "I'm having a wonderful time, and I want to share it with you." Sensuality is generous.

A friend of mine once had a co-worker named Betsy. Betsy was pleasant-looking, but her nose was actually a little too big for her face, and she had her fair share of wrinkles. However, after my friend and her husband took Betsy to dinner, the husband remarked to my friend that Betsy was just about the sexiest woman he'd ever met. My friend's marriage was quite secure, so she wasn't threatened by his remark, only puzzled. What in the world was sexy about Betsy? She wasn't gorgeous, her figure wasn't perfect, and she wasn't walking around in four-inch heels and hotpants, either.

And then it dawned on her: Betsy loved life and loved people. When Betsy was with someone, her attitude seemed to say, "You're the most important person in the world, and I love being with you."

That's sensuality, girls. And sensuality—and the true sexiness it produces—lasts. If your sexiness is simply external, you can't hold on to it forever. But, sensuality, well, that can last you a lifetime, enriching not only your experiences, but the lives of many others.

*Sex, Boys
& You:
Be Your
Own Best
Girlfriend*

110

PHOTO BY KAREN BOWERS

More space follows to write your thoughts,
or to write to Joni.

Joni Arredia
c/o Perc Publishing
P.O. Box 351030
Toledo, Ohio 43635

CHAPTER EIGHT

Street Smarts

STREET SMARTS, some are born with it and others have to learn through trial and error. But we all must learn! The three E's are vitally important. **Eyes and Ears, Everywhere.** Best advice— gently remind yourselves of the 3 E's every single time you walk out a door. Every situation is an unknown and full of surprises. Be smart, have fun, but don't be caught off guard or, as the old cliché goes, "with your pants down!"

These are good guidelines for you to use for the rest of your life and to pass on with love. I know, I know, you might have heard them before, but a gentle reminder always helps and never hurts.

Next, I have compiled a great list of 800 phone numbers you can call that are free from any phone. Always remember to dial the (1) first. Also, with computers becoming a huge source of communication, I thought you might enjoy having some valuable websites. We all like to communicate in different ways. What's important here is that we keep on communicating!

At the tip of your fingers you now possess an extraordinary log. You can use this to find out important information or just to get help or advice from people in the know. If you need help, just ask. That's why these numbers and web sites are available. Don't be afraid, instead, be smart. Ask, and you shall receive. It's amazing how well that works!

Use this information for yourself, a friend, or a perfect stranger in need. Remember, knowledge is power. This will help you to be your own best girlfriend.

1. Don't answer the door without verifying who it is, even if you are expecting your best friend. If a person claims to be someone you know and you *do not,* have them return when an adult is home.

2. When returning home, anytime day or night, be aware and **Pay Attention** to your surroundings, people, cars etc., before you open the door.

3. Close the door **tightly** whenever you are in your home, or any home alone, and **use** all locks provided.

4. Never give your *real* phone number when making a purchase. Make up a fake phone number, I do it all the time. You don't want strangers at the cash register or in the store to hear it and use it.

5. Do not draw attention to yourself in public places by displaying cash, jewelry, purse or wallet contents. Perfect strangers can quickly eyeball your phone number and address off your ID and use it!

6. Don't **ever** invite strangers into your car or home.

7. Do not leave valuables visible in your vehicle. Keep your valuables invisible and locked up in the trunk or glove compartment. Always lock your car. Upon returning to your vehicle, immediately begin looking around, under, and in your car before entering it.

8. Do not leave your keys and your possessions in your vehicle while filling up your gasoline tank. The same holds true when paying for the gas.

9. If you see any suspicious activity, report your observations. Call 911! It's called a Random Act of Kindness for others and Street Smarts for YOU.

10. Never shop alone after dark. Use the buddy system— it's more fun that way! If it's an absolute must to go alone, be sure to park in a well lit area and keep your eyes and ears everywhere. Walk quickly with head tall, back straight and eyes forward to give you the look of "being on a mission!"

Hotlines for Help

Here the list of important numbers to keep in your hip pocket. Help is just a phone call or a keyboard away!

Alcohol & Drug Abuse

Al-Anon & Alatee
www.al-anon.alateen.org
1-800-356-9996

National Clearinghouse for Alcohol & Drug Info
www.health.org
1-800-SAY-NOTO

National Cocaine Hotline
www.DRUGHELP.org
1-800-262-2463

National Council on Alcoholism and Chemical
Dependency Hope Line
1-800-622-2255

National Institute on Drug Abuse Hotline
www.DRUGHELP.org
1-800-662-HELP

Child Abuse

Boys Town
www.btnews.boystown.org
1-800-448-3000

Child Help USA National Child Abuse Hotline
www.childhelpusa.org
1-800-422-4453

National Coalition Against Domestic Violence
www.inetport.com~ndvh
1-800-799-7233

Health & HIV/AIDS

AIDS Action Council & Foundation
www.aidsaction.org
1-202-986-1300

AIDS Clinical Trials Information Service
www.actis.org
1-800-TRIALS-A

American Foundation for AIDS Research (AmFar) www.amfar@amfar.org	1-212-682-7440
Ask A Nurse	1-800-535-1111
Gay Men's Health Crisis www.gmhc.org	1-212-807-6655
National AIDS Hotline www.cdcnac.org	1-800-342-AIDS
National AIDS Hotline (Spanish Language)	1-800-344-SIDA
National AIDS Hotline (Hearing Impaired)	1-800-AIDS-TTY
National AIDS Information Clearinghouse www.cdcnac.org	1-800-458-5231
National Foundation for Cancer Research www.nfcr.org	1-800-321-CURE
National Health Information Center http://nhic-nt.health.org	1-800-336-4797
National Pediatric HIV Resource Center www.pedhivaids.org	1-800-362-0071
Office of Minority Health Resource Center	1-800-444-MHRC
California AIDS Hotline www.staf.org	1-415-863-AIDS
National STD Hotline www.ashastd.org	1-800-227-8922

National Child Welfare Organizations

Child Find of America www.dlinder@aol.com	1-800-I-AM-LOST
Child Quest International Sighting Line www.childquest.org	1-800-248-8020

Literacy Hotline/Dept. of Education	1-800-228-8813
National Center for Missing & Exploited Children	1-800-843-5678
Kids Save Line www.kidspeace.org	1-800-KID-SAVE
National Teenline	1-800-522-TEEN

Pregnancy

Planned Parenthood	1-800-230-7526
America's Crisis Pregnancy Hotline www.thehelpline.org	1-800-672-2296

Runaways Hotlines

Covenant House Nineline www.covenanthouse.org	1-800-999-9999
National Runaway Switchboard www.nrscrisisline.org	1-800-621-4000

Sex, Boys
& You:
Be Your
Own Best
Girlfriend

120

Who else might you want to call, or just talk to?

CHAPTER NINE

The Two Things All Women Want

No, this is not a chapter about two guys who are the current hot heartthrobs. Nor is it about success and fame. Or even bigger breasts and tighter buns.

This chapter is about safety and acceptance. You want them now, and you'll want them as long as you live.

Be Smart: Be Safe

Your need for safety is big, very big. Sad, but true. As a woman, you have the capacity for the emotional strength of a Mother Theresa. Physically, you have the strength to someday deliver a baby. (They don't call it *labor* for nothing.) What you lack, however, because of anatomical differences between men and women, is upper body strength.

Unfortunately, that makes you physically vulnerable in a world that is increasingly violent.

But, that doesn't mean you have to be a victim, not if you use your head and take time to be safe.

Be aware of everything going on around you. If you're walking down the street and see a fight going on, turn around and find an alternative route to your destination. Don't go to the mall alone at night. Let somebody know where you're supposed to be at all times. If your parents are having a huge fight and getting violent, stay out of the middle of it: **lots** of girls get injured trying to separate their parents. And, if you're attacked, scream FIRE! Some people turn their heads from a cry of "Help!" but few ignore the threat of fire.

I wish I'd been aware of the need for safety when I was thirteen. I was walking home from a ball game at dusk with three girlfriends. We were too busy having a good time to pay attention to what was going on around us. Suddenly, five older boys jumped us. They felt us up, pushed us around, and struck us with a big whip—no joke! At one point, they held one of my friends over the river and threatened to drop her. These guys were not kidding around. My friends and I fought and screamed and kicked and cried, and finally got away. Even in that kinder, gentler time of my girlhood, not one car stopped to help us. We went door to door until a sweet little old lady let us in and called one of our moms to pick us up. This also goes to prove there is not always safety in numbers, especially if no one is paying attention.

I'm telling you this story so you'll be wiser, more aware of your surroundings. You have to make safety happen. For most of your life, adults have made it happen for you, but as you grow older, it's your responsibility.

How Do You Rate on the Safety Scale?

1. You're walking down the street when you see a bunch of creepy-looking guys at the next corner. They notice you and start walking towards you. You…

   a. Walk into the nearest store and tell a clerk what's happening, then call the police.

   b. Run into a deserted building.

   c. Pull out your .357 Magnum and fire away.

2. When you return to your car at the mall, you…

   a. Walk confidently, have the key out and ready, look under the car before you reach it, and check out the back seat before you get inside.

   b. Trail fifty-dollar bills out of your purse while walking with your hands full.

   c. Start screaming, "So you think you can take me, Punks?"

3. You're taking a plane to see your grandparents and you're traveling alone. When you have a two-hour layover at the Chicago Airport, you…

   a. Stay in public areas and remain aware of what's going on around you.

   b. Find a deserted little spot and get lost in a good book.

   c. Hitch a ride to the city's most crime-ridden neighborhood in search of action.

Your score:
- If your answers are mainly a's, you've got a good perspective on safety.
- If you answered mostly b's, you've either got a death wish, or you need to be a whole lot more safety-conscious.
- If you answered mainly c's, you're Arnold Schwarzenegger.

So, keep your eyes and ears perked! Sure, there are places you can relax and let your guard down, but when you're out and about, know who's around and what's happening. In other words, develop your street smarts, the 3 E's, and save yourself from major league trauma.

Friends and Safety

Once you begin to think about safety, you may find yourself reconsidering who you want to hang with. **Pay attention** to your friends' habits and those of the people they hang with. Do they drive too fast? Do they drink and drive? Do drugs? Swim in that old, abandoned quarry pond with all the junked cars and no trespassing signs around it? If what your friends want to do poses a threat to your safety, you can still be friendly, but just "too busy" to hang out with them. It's always better to be alone than to get yourself in situation that could turn out to be all wrong for you.

Don't Sell Out for Acceptance

This brings us to acceptance. As women, we all want it and strive for it. Geez—many times we'll even change our beliefs and forego our dreams to get it. We may be tempted to lie and cheat to be accepted into what everyone else considers the cool group or gang.

Wrong. Dead wrong.

When that happens, you lose all sense of yourself and who you are. You're totally confused, and worse, you become just like everybody else: clones. At the time, it seems so important to be part of the group, but you've got to keep your eye on the big picture of your life.

Sex, Boys
& You:
Be Your
Own Best
Girlfriend

126

So, when you feel like sacrificing what you believe in to fit in, take a giant step backwards and look at what's happening, sort of like you're watching a movie. Play it out in your mind: if the "heroine"—that's you—deserts her dreams or endangers herself to be a part of the group, what's the ending of this movie likely to be? Then ask yourself honestly if that's where you want to be.

Doing this isn't real easy: at the time it seems a lot easier to go along with everyone else. You don't want to be a misfit: you want acceptance. But, being a misfit can be an asset if we decide to view it that way.

The Glories of Being Different

Misfits are true individuals. And I believe, in that sense, that being a misfit is a good thing. Isn't it incredible when you get attention because of what's unique about you?

Part of the problem is the word itself: *misfit*. It implies that something's wrong with you—when absolutely nothing is. You're a maverick: independent, self-styled. You've got the ability and the guts to put your stamp on the world, not the other way around. Put that way, isn't being a misfit delectable?

Madonna apparently thinks so. She's a woman who does exactly what's right for her and could care less what anyone thinks. Did you ever think about her that way? Probably not. You see her as cool, ahead of the pack, in style, bold. But, what makes her that way is that she's a misfit, an original, and there's no one else on the face of the earth exactly like her.

Was it easy for a young girl from Michigan to become the world-famous Madonna? I don't think so. She fought her way to the top, guided by her dream of being a success. I imagine there were many times people made fun of her for being different. But today, even those who don't care for her style can admire her determination.

If You Think You're a Misfit, You're Not Alone. Every woman I know thinks there are ways in which she doesn't fit in. That includes women who are beautiful, popular, successful—the last females on earth you'd consider misfits. I'll bet that if you could get the most popular girl in school to "fess up," you'd discover that she feels like a misfit at least part of the time. If you are the most popular girl in school, you know that's true. That's why it's important to support one another as we pursue our dreams, different as they may be. Let's make it a goal to celebrate and respect our differences.

Peer Pressure: Is It Really?

You also have to recognize something very important in your search for acceptance, and that's peer pressure. Adults talk about this all the time: "Kids are under so much peer pressure," they say. "No wonder they get in trouble." But I don't think that's the case all the time.

Oh, sure, there are some real jerks who will dare you to walk across a train trestle on stilts while blindfolded, but you've probably got the sense to recognize that they *are* jerks. And there are times that you'll have to make a stand and say "no" to something the other kids are doing.

However, most of the time, I think that instead of peer pressure, what you're really facing is your *belief* that other kids expect you to do something or act a certain way, when the truth is, they're so busy worrying about themselves that

Sex, Boys
& You:
Be Your
Own Best
Girlfriend

128

they're not even thinking about you. People of all ages act on the basis of what they **believe** to be true, not necessarily what is true. We all do this, even when it comes to ourselves. Is it peer pressure or perception?

How often does a friend worth having actually say "If you don't stay out all night with me, I'll hate you forever?" Instead, isn't it your own insecurity that makes you afraid she'll hate you? Or, when you tell your parents you simply have to do something because everyone else is. Do you really know for certain that *everyone* is doing it? Or, are you letting your fear of being a misfit assume that everyone but you is cool?

I think if you really look at this issue, you'll find that a good deal of the time you're putting a whole lot more pressure on yourself to conform than anyone else ever could. In other words, it's not so much that you actually face peer pressure. It's that you *think* you face peer pressure.

It's Vital to Accept Yourself

Do you know why you worry so much about what everyone else thinks? Because you don't have all the self-acceptance you need. If you don't have self-acceptance—or self-esteem, self-confidence, or whatever else you want to call it—no amount of acceptance from others can make up for it.

So, how do you accept yourself? Focus on what you **can** do, not on what you can't. Concentrate on your positives, not your negatives. Develop your muliebrity, those qualities and powers you possess as a female.

I had to do that—but first I had to realize I could do it—especially since I'd been sexually abused. If you've been abused, you know what I mean. As victims, our femininity, our softness, beauty, and purity have been ripped from us. We feel tainted, dark, dirty and ugly. Mostly we feel unworthy. But, let's stop right there, girls.

Perhaps you've been abused. Perhaps you haven't, but you still doubt your worth.

Never, ever, let what someone else thinks of you, or does to you, determine what you think of yourself. A feeling of worth comes from within. I didn't learn this until my thirties, so I want to pass this knowledge to you now, so you don't waste years of wondering, wandering, and making poor choices like I did. I want you to build a solid foundation of self-acceptance, then use your positives, your skills, and your muliebrity to build upon it and achieve your dreams.

There's nothing wrong with wanting to be accepted by others. But, it's more important to accept yourself, hang onto your dreams—and stay safe in the process.

Sex, Boys
& You:
Be Your
Own Best
Girlfriend

130

Perfect Strangers.
Perfect Friends.

I LEARNED MUCH of what I know about life and love from my parents and my husband. But, I also learned it from other people in life. Some of them were friends. Some of them were strangers. At every stage of my learning, those from whom I learned were the perfect teachers for the job. Perfect Strangers, Perfect Friends.

Peggy

My first Perfect Friend was Peggy. I was four, and shy, pathetically shy, but Peggy was my friend.

Peggy lived on our street, and every day I went to Peggy's back door—but didn't ring the doorbell. I just stood there and waited to see if someone would notice me, this very quiet, slight, dark, curly-headed little girl. Then ever so slowly and softly I called Peggy's name, finally mustering the courage to get louder and louder until someone came to the door. Peggy was my friend, because Peggy was always glad to see me. She made me smile.

My time with Peggy was freedom from the ugliness, from being forced by That Boy to do things no child should ever even know about. Together, she and I walked to kindergarten, and played in the neighborhood. She was someone I could count on. Peggy was a comforter, a nurturer, and my very first Perfect Friend.

But, fortunately, not the last.

My Beautiful Kindergarten Teacher

As I've said, I was shy at four. I couldn't look anyone in the eye, largely because of my incredible fear that the whole world knew what was happening to me. So, you can imagine what a trauma starting kindergarten was for me. And to make it worse, my birthday was in November, so I was sent to school when I was just four. However, it was somewhat bearable because Peggy and I walked there together.

Until that horrible morning when I was running late—and Peggy went to school without me.

I froze when Mom said I had to walk to school by myself. I sobbed and pleaded to stay home, but to no avail. I was sent out into the chilly morning, and cried all the way to school, questioning where I would find the strength to walk into school late. Since I couldn't come up with a satisfactory answer, I didn't walk into that forbidding brown building. I sat outside on the steps instead.

Sex, Boys
& You:
Be Your
Own Best
Girlfriend

136

Eventually, the morning chill gave way to the warmth of a brilliant sun. I remember thinking that I was alone on the steps, and that the sun was alone in the sky, and suddenly its warmth flowed through me, and I burst into song, that famous song, "Somewhere Over the Rainbow." Sometime during my third or fourth encore, as I hovered between reality and Oz, I was touched by the second Perfect Friend of my young life.

My beautiful kindergarten teacher came outside and stood by me. She smiled, and put her hand out for me to hold. I didn't speak, and neither did she. Somehow, she knew that I was afraid to enter my classroom. We walked hand in hand into that big kindergarten room and I felt cozy and warm. No more fear. And so, from that second Perfect Friend, I learned more lessons about love, namely, the quiet strength of kindness.

I learned about the beauty of a woman's intuition, the comfort of touch, and the strength of silence.

Strangers Who Teach

I've learned so much from Perfect Strangers. From a young deaf man I met in New York City when I was still a girl, I learned patience. When I was twenty-two, Chuck and I were on our honeymoon in Hawaii, and I was greatly inspired by the attitude of a delightful young mother I observed for just fifteen minutes as she interacted with her children: loving and laughing with them, completely immersed in the moment. She was a shining example of a warm woman and a nurturing mother. The parenting lessons I learned from that Perfect Stranger are with me yet today.

Perfect Strangers. Perfect Friends.

I Was the Greatest Star

One of the greatest lessons I learned from a Perfect Stranger took place when I was thirteen and saw the movie, *Funny Girl*. I so admired the way Barbra Streisand played the part of Fanny Brice that shy, retiring, afraid-to-open-her-mouth me decided to pantomime "I Am the Greatest Star" for a special project we had at school.

I practiced for weeks. I had the costume, the attitude, and the moves. When I performed in front of my class, I brought the house down for the very first time in my life. My teacher, Sister Char, gave me an A+ for that project. It was my first A+ ever! I will always be grateful to Barbra Streisand, that Perfect Stranger, for helping me take some of my earliest steps towards overcoming those demons of shyness and shame that had plagued me throughout my young life. When I read her autobiography years later, I discovered that Ms. Streisand had her own demons to face, and acting in *Funny Girl* was integral to the process. Funny, as I write this, I realize that that A+ has led me throughout my working career. The stage continues still to be my favorite place!

Tony Tuna

Years later, before I married, I made another very special Perfect Friend, whom I nicknamed Tony Tuna. As you know, because I had been sexually abused, dating was scary.

After high school, I took off in a VW bug with a friend, and traveled from Ohio to California. I wanted to be a star. However, I settled in Berkeley, not Hollywood. Instead of becoming a star, I learned some truths about men, women, and the true nature of real love. All in all, probably a better bargain than stardom.

My older sister knew some sailors who lived in Berkeley, and my friend and I moved into their house. Those sailors acted like big, gentle brothers, and they watched out for us both, which was a very good thing indeed. Our naïveté was obvious to everyone but us. We, of course, considered ourselves women of the world, having traveled cross-country by ourselves via Volkswagen. From those dear, kind sailors I learned an awful lot about how nice men can really be.

Tony Tuna was one of the nicest, a true southern gentleman. He must have seen the terror in my eyes and sensed the horror in my heart when it came to a male-female relationship. So, he was very patient and kind, this Perfect Stranger.

We played together every day, Tony and I. We swam in the ocean, jumped off cliffs, walked, danced, shopped, cleaned house, played tag, held hands, and enjoyed just being silly. All the things I should have done as an innocent child.

Slowly, I began to trust a man, this man. We were falling in love.

This Perfect-Stranger-become-Perfect-Friend taught me that love is gentle. That it shelters, protects, and never, ever bruises, scars, or threatens. Above all, love gives rather than takes.

I haven't heard from Tony Tuna since he sailed out of my life that summer long ago. But, in my heart of hearts, I know that somewhere in the world there is one very happy woman sharing her life with that gentle, dear man who taught me my first lessons about the nature of love between a man and a woman. Tony managed to give me back some of my

*Perfect
Strangers.
Perfect
Friends.*

childhood, and he also helped me begin to understand about true womanhood.

After Tony, men floated in and out of my life. And, despite my experience with him, for a long time, I still felt I had to control my relationships.

That was both a wonderful and horrible time in my life. I was single and broke, barely surviving on my salary as a bank teller, but always having a great time. I had several friends in the same situation, so we all took care of one another— another lesson learned about love. Those single years were a very generous time.

My Chuck

It took a while after Tony Tuna, yet the most magnificent Perfect Stranger eventually walked into my life. As I write this, Chuck and I have been married for nearly twenty years, and he's become the most Perfect Friend I've ever had.

Chuck's love changed forever the still somewhat cynical view I had of male-female relationships when I met him. His love has nurtured me, and helped me grow into the woman I am today. He finished the lessons Tony Tuna started, proving to me once and for all that love is not selfish, but gives, and gives, and gives. Chuck shared that love is patient, always bearing with me when I'm driven by my past to strike out or retreat in fear. Chuck has taught me the healing power of selfless love, and inspired me to pass that love on to others.

Be a Perfect Stranger or Perfect Friend

That kind of love takes time. But remember, girls, that it is in our bones to love and serve one another. Look for opportunities to be a Perfect Stranger or a Perfect Friend.

When the stranger ahead of you in the movie ticket line sneezes, bless her. Don't be too busy to help your friends. Make time to volunteer, to teach a child to read, to visit a lonely widow, or to serve meals to the homeless. Also, never fail to let your family know how much you cherish them.

Make it a habit to pay attention to all those around you and love will flow through you, unforced, easy, and beautiful. Love will then return to bless you a thousand times over.

Perfect Stranger:
A lesson learned from afar.

Perfect Friend:
Someone who expects nothing in return.

You can have both.
You can be both.

Perfect Strangers. Perfect Friends.

CHAPTER ELEVEN

IT'S ALL IN THE

Packaging

AT THIS POINT IN YOUR LIFE, the way you look is A Huge Priority. That's because you think if you look cool, you'll be accepted. You just might attract that special guy, too.

Know what?

You're right, in some respects. If you wear the "right" clothes, if you've got a great body, and your hair always looks good, then other kids see you as cool, hip. If you dress geeky, or you're hair is as different as mine was at your age, then you seem uncool and nerdy. In other words, the way you dress is another way to be in control—you're controlling how people react to you.

That can be good. But, it's not enough. This next example illustrates what I mean.

Take Your Cue from Encino Man

Have you ever seen the movie *Encino Man?* In it, two teenage boys dig up a frozen caveman—actually, a cave teen—by accident. Once they defrost him, they dress him up in hip clothes, cut his hair, and tell their parents that he's an exchange student. Of course, he doesn't speak or understand English, but he looks cool, so he's accepted by all the kids at school. In fact, he's elected prom king.

Since he looks the part—like he **should** fit in—he **does** fit in, even though he's totally clueless.

Later, everyone gets to know Encino Man. All the girls fall in love with him because he has no airs, no hang-ups, no ego. He doesn't have the slightest idea how to be cool: he only knows how to be Encino Man. However, his outer packaging invited people to look on the inside and discover the real him.

Fanny Brice, the "Funny Girl" Barbra Streisand portrayed in that film I love so much, once said, "Let the world know you as you are, not as you think you should be, because sooner or later, if you are posing, you will forget the pose, and then where are you?"

You're right in thinking that if you wrap your inner self in an attractive package, people will want to take a closer look at you. So go ahead: do up your package as attractively as you know how. Have fun! Even get wild and crazy! But, always remember to be true to yourself on the inside. No matter how great the package looks on the outside, the very best part should be what's inside, and it will be, as long as you have the confidence to be yourself.

*Sex, Boys
& You:
Be Your
Own Best
Girlfriend*

144

Dressing the Part

At a very young age, I discovered that dress was a way to be totally me, apart from everyone else.

Of course, it took years to be able to dress with finesse. Some of the get-ups I put together during those learning years would make your hair stand on end! But, good or bad, it was still my look, solely and completely mine.

Clothes were my armor. You see, I only wanted people to see the outside package: no way did I want anyone to see the *real* me inside: hurt, depressed, terrified, ashamed, and so painfully shy. All these feelings were a result of the sexual abuse I suffered for so long. And it worked! The way I dressed caused others to believe I was attractive, and so they treated me as if I were, even though I felt ugly and used inside.

Through that experience, I learned—like Encino Man—that clothes give us the ability to dress a part, reflect that facet of our personality we're in the mood to display on any given day. The way we dress can be a tremendous help when we're learning about who we are and the image we want to project.

Are you creative and want it to show? Break out the colorful, flowing, retro-hippie duds.

Into being seen as serious? Try wearing black and get your hands on a pair of classic specs. Want others to see you as cutting-edge? Go for trendy. You get the idea.

Clothes are our costumes. When I think *costumes*, I think of parties. Oftentimes, gifts are given at parties. Don't you look forward most to opening the packages that are brilliantly wrapped? You know the kind: shiny, shimmering paper, tons of ribbon tied in extra big bows, with a bauble attached to tease us. We know there must be something grand inside to warrant such incredible packaging.

If you have the right attitude, life can be a party. The costumes you wear to the party of life can act as gift wrap that makes others want to know more about what lies inside. That gift wrap—the way you dress—can provide an enticing glimpse of the person you are.

And, if you've not quite yet become the person you want to be, then dressing the part—wrapping the package to reflect your dreams—can give you the confidence to continue on until you have actually become what you want to be.

Discovering Your Style

When you first start experimenting with clothes and makeup and hair, you may feel you look goofy. Hang in there. This is how you learn what works for you.

I'm not going to kid you: sometimes your experiments may get laughed at. I know mine did. I wish it weren't so, but kids do tend to laugh, so be prepared. Better yet, laugh with them. They'll appreciate your being a good sport, and they may even turn around and copy what you did because you had the confidence to carry your look off with such style and good humor. Remember what I said earlier—-imitation is the highest form of flattery!

Some women I know have one look and they stick with it, because that's what works for them. Others, like me, have lots of different looks. Right now is a good time in your life to try all the looks you can. If you try a look and it doesn't work or you just don't feel comfortable in it, try to figure out what went wrong. Sometimes it's because you didn't get the look

Sex, Boys
& You:
Be Your
Own Best
Girlfriend

146

quite right. Other times, it's because the look simply isn't you.

As you experiment, you need to remember that not everyone will agree with your style, your choices.

So what?

It's *your* image. They're *your* choices. If you feel right about them, and they're not different to the point of being offensive, don't be concerned about everyone else. Don't let a negative comment make you change what you know is right for you. When you feel good in your costume, and comfortable with your style, then you will automatically stand taller, and feel more confident. People will pay attention to you, and then, like magic, your world will begin to change.

Experiment with the way you dress and wear your hair. Try on something new and different, just because *you* want to. Then go out and strut your stuff. Do it just for fun, like you did when you played dress-up as a little kid. Step out of your comfort zone: remember—courage to change!

Packaging Strategies

What if you don't have two cents to rub together to buy clothes. What do you do then? Share with your cousins, sisters, mom, aunt, and grandma. Ask mom or your older sister to take you to the second-hand store: the selection is terrific and the prices can't be beat. Take turns with your friends cleaning out each others' closets, then trade stuff. What's old to you is new to them, and vice versa.

Always be sure to dress for the occasion. Know where you're going and what kind of people will be there, then dress accordingly, in your own beautiful style. There's a time and

What you see in the mirror and what others see are two different things. You see just your reflection; your friends see your walk, posture, mannerisms—the whole picture of who you are.

*It's All
in the
Packaging*

147

place for all the different types of clothing you love to wear. You may want to stand out in the crowd, but let it be because you've got the neatest appropriate look, not because you're the only one wearing torn jeans at a formal wedding reception.

Try to put one trendy, hip-looking piece with every outfit you wear. All you need is one and you'll always look current. A pair of trendy shoes can work. So can the hottest color, or a great looking hat—especially on a bad hair day.

When it comes to hair, a good cut is Instant Hip. So, stay on top of that, and spend a little bit of money on keeping your hair in shape. If you're like I was, you'll color and straighten and cut and grow your hair a zillion times between now and adulthood: again, it's all a part of discovering who you are and what works for you. Besides, hair always grows out. Which brings me to my next point.

Go Wild—But Don't Go Permanent

Stepping out with clothes, jewelry, hair, and makeup is always fun, exciting and crazy. Part of the fun is that if it doesn't work, you can change it. What you *can't change* without a great deal of scarring and expense are tattoos. Been there. Done that.

When I was seventeen, I wanted to do what none of my friends had done, so I got a tattoo. My friend and I went to the tattoo parlor, and for five dollars, I had a tattoo drilled— and I mean *drilled*—on my chest. Let me explain how it's done in case you're thinking about having it done.

Because I wasn't into drugs, I went perfectly straight, and no one there even mentioned giving me a painkiller. The tattoo man took a small electric drill with a needle inserted in the end, dipped the needle in some ink, then proceeded to drill the needle into my tender, young, beautiful skin.

Talk about pain! It was the worst. And I'd *wanted* this?!

I started screaming, shaking, and crying, and all this creep did was tell me I wanted this, so I should sit still so he didn't mess up. Like a fool, I did what I was told, because I was too embarrassed to admit I'd made a major mistake. He ended screwing up anyway: what was supposed to be a teensy little pink flower ended up looking like a huge, ugly black star. But that was just the beginning of my problems.

I managed to hide my tattoo from my parents for months—until bathing suit season. Even then, I tried. But finally, my Mom saw it, and she absolutely freaked. "Why would you purposely scar your body for the rest of your life this way, Joni?" You could have cut the tension in our house with a knife that afternoon.

When Dad came home that day, he said, "You did it, so you must like it; now, I want you to show it off." Cool dad, right?

Wrong.

He knew I wasn't proud of it. He also knew the reactions I'd get from people, especially from strangers. There used to be a stigma attached to tattoos—maybe there still is. Back then, they told the world you were hard and tough. Neither of which I was, or wanted to be. What had I done?

Fortunately, I could hide my mistake under tops. Until the day when I was twenty and a great guy asked me to an elegant restaurant (the kind we all dream of going to with a handsome guy someday). I got all dressed up in the only fancy dress I owned, and it revealed a tiny glimpse of that awful tattoo. So my date saw it, and his entire attitude toward me was different after that. He told me point blank that it didn't fit my personality. It certainly didn't fit the elegant sophistication of this man or the wonderful restaurant we were in.

Suddenly, the light went off in my head. What was hip as a teenager wasn't so cool as I was getting older and my tastes were changing. So, just three short years after I had it put on, I had my tattoo surgically removed. Removing it, however, cost hundreds of dollars, and I now have another larger scar slightly different than my skin tone. At least that scar doesn't dictate what I am in the eyes of others.

So, think long and hard before you do something to your body that's permanent. A tattoo might be cool now, but in ten or twenty years, it could put you in a time warp—sort of like when you go to somebody's house and they've got gold and avocado kitchen appliances, and suddenly you're back in the Seventies.

What about all the body piercing that's going on these days? If you have pierced ears or know someone who does, take a look at that little scar it leaves: it is noticeable. Before you have multiple ear piercings, or have your tongue, nose, belly button, or eyebrow pierced, ask yourself if you're going to want those scars permanently. Really give it some thought, because permanently means forever—your entire life.

As you grow, your wants and desires change, too, so don't lock yourself into one look you have to live with for the rest of your life. Don't throw away that freedom to change your look in the future. Do anything you want that you can change later: dye your hair green, shave your head. Wear black nail polish. Get outrageous with a deep purple, sparkled, iridescent eyeshadow look. Get absolutely crazy with your clothes. Just don't do something you can't change, because chances are you'll wish you could in just a few years.

The Two Absolutely Essential Accessories

You can spend tons of money on clothes, and work on your hair and makeup for hours, but if you fail to **smile** and display less-than-confident **posture,** your entire look can be ruined.

Posture is attitude. It's how you present yourself, your stance. If you have a smashing, drop-dead outfit, show you love it by standing tall. Take a deep breath, fill your lungs full. Try it! You look in command. On the other hand, walk into a room with rounded shoulders and your head slung low, and you look scared and pathetic.

If you think you're too tall and you slink down to look shorter, you won't fool anyone—you'll just look like a slouchy tall person. Besides, think of all those supermodels who are six feet tall. If you're rounding your shoulders to hide the fact that you're the first girl on your block with a bosom—well, that doesn't work, either. You end up looking like a girl with a bosom and a posture problem. Instead, stand up straight and strut your stuff. There's a whole bunch of us flat-chested types who are downright envious of what you've got.

Whatever you do, smile—it's the bright, beautiful bow on that gorgeous package that's you.

You know how sometimes you feel incredibly self-conscious, like everyone's looking at you? The minute you smile, you're telling the world that you think you look terrific, and when you do that, the world's likely to believe you. You do something else with that smile: you take the focus off yourself and reach out to all those other kids who are also feeling self-conscious. By smiling, you say, "Hey, I like you." When you do that, you help build their confidence, and they're bound to like you for that.

Smile, and everybody wins.

I remember when I first started using makeup, I went way overboard. I think we have a tendency when we're young to do that, and that's okay. However, be sure your look is who you really are. Put all that makeup together with that wiggle in your walk you're learning and too-tight clothes, and you could end up being a fast-looking girl, just like I was. Is that the real you? Could you soften your look a bit to better match your personality?

*Sex, Boys
& You:
Be Your
Own Best
Girlfriend*

152

Helping You Become the Person You Want to Be

Clothes, makeup, and hair are powerful tools that can help us explore a range of possibilities as we work our way to personal fulfillment. Our outer costume builds our inner confidence, and as our confidence grows, it, in turn, shows itself in costumes that are increasingly "us."

It's freeing—and it's so much fun!

Dress your outer self to reveal the beauty of your soul. Let your soul be made increasingly beautiful as it draws confidence from the way you dress. You've heard of *vicious* circles? This circle is anything but. This is a circle of growth and love. What results from it is a magical gift with an outer edge as lovely as the inner beauty it cradles.

Trust me when I say, girls, that this wonderful gift, so beautifully packaged, can be you.

CHAPTER TWELVE

MAKING ALL THE RIGHT MOVES

I STARTED MY JOURNEY to happiness and fulfillment as a shy, introverted child in the early years of elementary school. As I told you earlier, the first step on that path came in the form of exercise.

My story may not be like yours. My road to happiness started with externals: exercise, nutrition, clothes, and good deeds. They gave me confidence, and people responded to that confidence positively. After a while, their belief in me, their approval, reinforced my confidence and sense of self to the point that when the time came, I was able to face my past squarely in the face. More importantly, I was finally able to look inside myself, and begin to better develop those inner qualities of being female—muliebrity—that have contributed to the happiness and fulfillment I enjoy today.

Power Moves

I've already said that your path may not start with externals. However, I am going to make a strong pitch for exercise here, not because I think we all need to look like Cindy Crawford or any other thin, fit, famous model, actress, athlete or recording artist, but because exercise empowers us. It not only gives us physical strength: it gives us energy, and a sense of being comfortable in our body. It's also a wonderful way of blowing off stress.

Exercise is freedom—the freedom of movement. Exercise is action—an expression of body language. It provides a sensation of letting go and unwinding. There is something so basic about movement, and yet it makes you feel so unbelievably good. It's a way to hang onto the most important thing you can ever have in this world: your health.

Exercise for the Health of It

When you're young, you feel invincible, like nothing will ever happen to you. You'll always be young and strong. You'll always be healthy. But, you may not be if you don't exercise.

Think back to a time you were really sick with something horrible like the flu. Your body wasn't in good working order: you couldn't focus, couldn't concentrate, and didn't have any energy. Over time, if you don't take care of that body by exercising it, you may not be quite as bad as you were when you had the flu, but you sure won't feel on top of your game, either. The movement of exercise is what keeps you strong, healthy, alive, flexible and coordinated.

Establish the Exercise Habit

If you haven't already, make exercise a habit, like brushing your teeth. Actually, a better analogy is flossing. If you let your gums deteriorate, you lose your teeth. If you don't exercise your muscles, you lose your ability to move around freely, and perhaps forego your health. Most importantly, if you fail to exercise, you lose your mental edge, and miss a grand opportunity to build the confidence that comes from having control of your body.

You may cringe when you hear the word *exercise.* Remember discipline? You know it's something you *should* be doing, but some of you don't realize you need to do it consistently to reap its mental and physical benefits. And it's so darned hard to fit into your schedule.

But think, girls. How many different things do you have to do?

Everything! As females, you can juggle twenty different activities at once—and you do.

It's the blessing and the curse of the superior being that we are!

Ah, but to juggle them with an upbeat attitude, you have to be fit. Fitness gives you an edge, keeps you sharp, helps you maintain a sunny disposition, and helps you look at yourself in a brighter light. Exercise magnifies everything you touch, mainly because it clears our "cobwebs" or confusion in our minds.

Whatever you do, don't give up on exercise: its benefits *are* attainable if you're disciplined and consistent. If you do occasionally slip up, that's okay. Simply get up and try again and again and again.

No matter what your regimen, remember to smile. I'm convinced that it's the most beneficial exercise of all. It keeps us in the right frame of mind, and it keeps everyone else guessing. *How come she's having so much fun?*

Food for Thought

"It's munchie time. What to eat, what to eat. Do I eat? Should I eat? I'm fat. I have to lose weight. I can't eat. I'm on a diet. I'm starved, but I don't want to eat in front of anyone. Everybody is skinny but me. When I look in the mirror all I see is fat. I'm hungry all the time. I hide food in my room. How can I ever lose weight when food is everywhere? All I can think about is food. What am I going to eat next? I either eat too much or not at all. I have a headache. Oh, God, I just ate a whole bag of chips. I have to throw up. Maybe he'll like me better if I'm skinny."

Sound familiar?

That's because most of us have a love-hate relationship with food.

Either we hate food or we love food. Never has there been a nation of people so screwed up about the whole food issue. We either indulge ourselves to the point of exploding, or we starve ourselves. Whatever happened to moderation?

Right now, more than ever, you need to eat—and eat the right things. Your body and mind are growing at an incredible rate, and if you don't feed them, they starve. To be fast on your feet and mentally sharp and control of your destiny, you've got to eat. Strength comes from food.

Moderation, Moderation, Moderation

You've read a lot in these chapters about being the best you can be. I know that when I used to starve myself, I was far from my best: first I was mean, and then I was weak. I couldn't think straight. I lost all sense of balance and control because I was so hungry. I also know there are people on the other end of the spectrum who eat until they're so stuffed they can't move. There's a middle ground here, and you need to find it.

One of the best ways to do that is to listen to your body. Only eat when it says its hungry—not when you just want to eat, but when your body actually feels hungry. And then, listen to what your body says it needs. I mean, have you ever really thought about why you crave something? A craving for chips or pretzels may be your body's way of saying, "Hey, you, I'm low on salt." Sugar or chocolate? "Time for the old period." What about cheese or pizza? "I need protein, girl, and you haven't been eating a whole lot of it lately!"

Pay attention to your cravings, but no matter what, please make sure you eat energy food—plenty of vegetables and carbohydrates—and eat absolutely everything in moderation. A little bit of everything and not too much of any one thing. Mix it up with movement, and lots of water—a whole lot more water than soda pop.

I know, I know, water tastes like you-know-what. Nobody ever said it tasted good, but it is so good for you, and honestly, the more you drink, the better it will taste to you. Water helps keep your skin soft, and helps flush the bacteria from your body that just might be contributing to the zits you're probably getting now. Today—right now—make a habit of carrying bottled water wherever you go. Then just keep refilling the same bottle with more water. If it's the only liquid around to drink, you will drink it. It sure works that way for me!

Starving for Control

It's no coincidence that eating disorders are so common these days among girls your age. Our culture has made such a big deal about being thin that girls will do just about anything to be thin. Even starve themselves to the point of death (anorexia nervosa) or force themselves to throw up after they binge (bulimia). What's really sad is that lots of girls who are destroying themselves this way aren't really heavy: they just think they are.

Did you know that more than **90%** of the people sick with eating disorders are adolescent and young adult women? **Anorexia nervosa** affects girls between the **ages of 12-18.** Exactly the age of you girls reading *Sex, Boys & You!* This scary eating disorder develops in girls with low self-esteem who typically, but not always, come from white middle to upper middle class families. These families, in most cases, are full of high achievers and perfectionists who take pride in their physical appearance and how they look on the outside.

Of course, you want to look good. I do, too. But, you should realize that if you starve yourself—as opposed to eating sensibly—eventually it will take its toll on your body, and you will look tired and old before your time. I know that there are some of you right now who are living on three crackers a day and washing it down with water and working out and feeling great. But, that won't last forever. Honest. I wouldn't lie about this: it's too important. You can die from this disorder, really and truly.

So, how long before you collapse? Everyone in your family is worried. You think they're just jealous. Most of your friends don't have the guts to tell you how bad you look, but you hear the whispers behind your back. Having fun, are you?

You look in the mirror and all you see is a fat body because you've trained yourself to see nothing else. You're in charge, yessirree! You're showing everyone how strong you are, when in reality your body is slowly dying: you're so into this power game that you don't even feel it. Maybe you believe that life is so terrible that you don't care. But I'm telling you that I care!

If you have that kind of control, and everyone with an eating disorder does, don't use it to kill yourself: channel it into something that's good for you. If you've gone so far you can't turn around, then ask for help and do it now (look at Chapter 8). You'll probably find that people who care about you are just waiting for you to ask. Asking doesn't make you weak; it makes you **SMART.** No one in this life travels solo: we all need a helping hand at times. Please just ask. You are so worth it!

What's Eating You? And What Are You Eating?

What about those of you who find your only comfort in eating, and whose bodies grow larger as a result?

Keep in mind that eating for comfort, out of frustration, or for other emotional reasons can start you on the path to a lifetime of weight problems. Also remember that the biggest mistake you can make is to diet.

So, let's talk about diets, and why you shouldn't do them. The reason lies in the word itself: diet. *Die-et.*

That's precisely what your metabolism does—die—when you starve it.

Your metabolism is your engine, and food is the gasoline. You must feed your body to keep it fueled and running quickly and efficiently. Food keeps your metabolism moving at a rapid pace, burning up calories. Take it away, and your metabolism drops, and begins very, very slowly burning calories. Then you go off the diet, and go back to eating normally, and your metabolic rate is still tired from being starved of fuel, so it can't burn all those new-found calories. What happens? You gain weight faster. Bad news.

Diets kill your basic healthy instincts. They murder your happy attitudes, and bring you to the lowest mental and physical ebb. Here you are, trying to be your best, and diets have the opposite effect on you. They make you weak and irritable, unable to function, and they cause you to obsess about food and eat even more. Either way, you lose control of who you really are.

When I was an adolescent, I was on the Ayds candy plan— it was a diet plan before your time—trying to do battle with my body's natural tendency to "chunk up" for the growth spurt to come. Anyway, a little piece of Ayds candy, taken with a hot drink four times a day, was supposed to suppress my appetite. Instead, I was obsessed with food: I ate everything that wasn't tied down. Sound familiar? I decided right then and there never to diet again.

We die when we *die*-t. The word says it all, so please don't do it again. Take that word and throw it out of your vocabulary like you would any other four-letter word.

Instead of dieting, tell yourself to pick and choose rather than think in terms of deprivation. Don't be a slave to food. Do you love it? Yes, you do. Does it, or will you allow it, to control you? Absolutely not.

Get Real

The first step in adjusting your attitude towards food—whether you've been starving or stuffing yourself—is accepting your genetic heritage. The body we own is, for the most part, genetic. Take a look at your parents and the family album: what you see is probably pretty much what you'll get. Never, ever forget that. Of course you can tighten it, shrink it, harden it, soften it, but gals, love it with all your might. Stop trying to make it something it was never destined to be.

Those perfect-body models you see are just that: models. They represent a miniscule percentage of the population. They have someone prepping them for all their photo shoots, even taping and stapling on their clothes! And, as if that weren't enough, computers can now literally slice a few pounds off their photographed bodies. Imagine! Sculpted—although not real—thighs at the touch of a button!

Right now, you may think you need to look just like them. Unless you've got model-genes, it will never happen. Admire their beauty if you wish, but never buy into the idea that it's the only standard of beauty around.

I was blessed to be a franchise owner of a Jazzercise fitness business for thirteen years. Jazzercise was my vehicle! And boy, did I learn about myself and women in general. I used to watch women walk in the first time and hover in that back row, ready to make a quick exit. I understood, because I'd been there many times in my life, too.

So I zeroed in on every new face in a flash, doing everything in my power through my eyes, movement, and speech to make them feel as comfortable as possible— exactly what I would hope and pray someone would do for me. I knew that it took every bit of courage they could muster to get into a leotard, shorts, or whatever, drive to the facility, and walk through those doors: I remember psyching myself up to come to my very first class.

The miracle of it all was watching these beautiful Perfect Strangers change into the loveliest of butterflies. It was fascinating to watch the black clothing change into vibrant, self-assured, colored leotards. Hairstyles becoming more

Sex, Boys
& You:
Be Your
Own Best
Girlfriend

164

uplifting and trendy. The very best of all was the twinkle in their eyes, that brilliant sparkle that signaled the discovery of a woman they liked being.

Beautiful, bright, airborne butterflies. It was something that happened to every one of them over a period of four to six months.

*Did their bodies change? Maybe a little. But, more importantly, the way they **viewed** their bodies changed a lot. Their approach to life and to themselves became clear and focused. That's what taking time for yourself can do.*

What I treasure most from that time is what we all learned together—acceptance. Every one of us went through those doors the first time wanting to be a size six. Few of us got that, but that was okay. What we gained instead was more beauty than we could have ever imagined.

The beauty of companionship. Moderation. Learning to accept each others'—and our own—faults and differences. We learned that size doesn't dictate worth or beauty. We came to know that inner beauty gives us that outer edge we all desire, that confidence we need to make changes for the better.

Each of you has something totally unique, something that is yours, something those airbrushed models will never possess. Believe it! Find what is uniquely yours and build upon it.

Don't waste your time trying to be what you're not. No matter what you do, it will never be good enough. If you're obsessed with reaching that perfect weight or fitness level, you'll never be satisfied. Often, that's because you're trying for a look that your body type just can't achieve.

So, you became disappointed, over and over again. You blame yourself for lacking willpower, when it has nothing whatsoever to do with willpower.

On the contrary, I am always amazed at the willpower of overweight-underfit people who diet. Society treats these people as if they have no willpower, but that's not true. After all, they diet over and over again. Their willpower is amazing, because diets are just awful: they take incredible stamina and follow-through.

Let's talk about the really skinny people. The ones that never diet. The girls with just super high speed metabolisms. It's no picnic for them either. They have to listen to this kind of comment. "You make me so sick, you can eat what ever you want and stay skinny." Skinny girls get teased and picked on, too. Believe me when I say, they don't always like what they see in the mirror. Nor, do they like eating all the time just to keep their pants up! The grass is not always greener on the other side.

No matter what your weight is, you need to take your willpower and use it to your advantage. Apply it to something that will truly help you achieve physical and mental fitness. Stop thinking in terms of drastic measures that leave you weak, depressed, and discouraged. Instead, you need to set achievable, moderate goals that fit into your lifestyle and make you feel super.

Start Cutting Others Some Slack

Maybe you don't have a problem with food, but you've got problems with people who do. I used to. Eventually, I learned how wrong I was, and how much damage I was doing to the self-esteem of someone I loved because of it.

When my daughter, Lauren—incredibly bright, talented Lauren—hit puberty, she began to gain weight, just as I had when I was her age. I was so obsessed with what I considered her weight problem that I couldn't see her good qualities. All I saw was that my baby girl didn't look good. She was fat! She couldn't wear all those cute "in" clothes. So I harped and harped, and sometimes actually screamed because I was so angry with her. You know what all this did to my dear Lauren? That's right: she began eating even more on the sly.

Fortunately, a good friend helped me see what I was doing to my sweet girl. From that moment on, I zeroed in on Lauren's gifts. I stopped giving her those side glances that said I wasn't happy about the way she looked. I softened my eyes, my voice—and my thoughts.

My little girl started changing, too. As I demonstrated unconditional love (loving her no matter what) she began to feel worthy. Eventually, she decided to do something about her weight, all on her own.

It would have been okay if she hadn't decided to lose weight. What mattered most was that she had self-esteem. You can't allow yourself to go through life thinking—about yourself or

*Making
All the
Right Moves*

others—that you're okay except for that extra weight. You know, that you-have-such-a-pretty-face-and-you'd-be-so-much-better-off-if-you'd-lose-that-ugly-fat approach that colors your life and the lives of people around you until all becomes a discouraging shade of gray. I realize now that my negative attitude towards Lauren was a whole lot uglier than fat could ever be. We females are the absolute worst when it comes to this.

We belittle ourselves. We belittle others, if only in our minds. (How can she let herself look like that, we ask, and yet we don't know the first thing about who she is or how she got that way.) If we're that hung up on weight, if we're committing emotional murder with our thoughts, words, or attitudes, we have to stop it—right now.

Practice Positive Control

While I don't think we should be obsessed with food and weight, I do encourage everyone to exercise and practice good nutrition. Those things helped me in my journey to happiness, giving me a sense of control and well-being that prepared me to handle steps that came further down the road. If you're not practicing positive control in eating and exercise, ask yourself why.

When I was young, I hated to eat. I was so skinny I was nicknamed Joni Boney. I didn't understand that I was compensating for the loss of control during the abuse by gaining total control with my distaste for food. Once I understood this, I stopped practicing negative control—starving my body—and started practicing positive control, giving it what it needed to be healthy.

When you practice negative control, you eventually end up being its victim. Think about your friends who are anorexic or bulimic. They may have started out in charge, but eventually they can't help the fact that they're starving to death or throwing up after they eat: it's become an obsession. However, when you practice positive control, **you're** in charge.

So, ditch negative control and start practicing the positive variety. Get in touch with your body through exercise. Change your attitude toward food. These two actions can do near-miraculous things for you: they worked for me. I've seen them work for others.

I know they can work for you and help you become the best you that you can be. Your Own Best Girlfriend!

Look Above. Look in the Mirror.

Let the beauty we love be what we do.
There are hundreds of ways to kneel and kiss the ground.

– Rumi (Sufi poet)

THERE ARE two wonderful presents that you can give yourself as you make your journey through life. One is a good look in the mirror, not for the sake of admiring the package you come in, but for a deep look into the center of your soul. The other is a look—Above.

Connecting with a Higher Power

Because I was born to an Irish Catholic family and went to a Catholic school, I went to Church. Church became a refuge from That Boy's sick cruelties, a beautiful place where I discovered the strength of religion and God.

Church has always been my special spot, my quiet place. You need a place like that, too, and it doesn't have to be a church or any other place for religious worship. Just find a place where you can pull your thoughts together and take a good look at where you are, where you want to go, and how you're going to get there.

It was at Church that I learned that God loved me no matter what, and that was the consolation I needed so much during those fearful years of my childhood. There is nothing, nothing—no matter how bad it seems, that will make God stop loving you!

Yes, I believe that there is an Almighty Significant Other you can hold onto. One and the only one who does hear all your innermost thoughts. Whatever name you give the Supreme Being, I'm telling you to hang on tight to Him. That was vital to my own journey to happiness, and I think it's vital to yours, too.

So trust God—or whatever name you choose to call your Higher Power. And pray.

Prayer

Prayer is a wonderful way of communicating with God—and with ourselves. Nobody but you and your Almighty can hear. Prayer acts as a sounding board.

Some might refer to prayer as a form of meditation. Others might consider it a cleansing. The beauty of prayer is that we all manage to do it in as many different shapes and forms as exist among the bountiful clouds in the sky.

Prayer can be done anywhere, at any time, but we seem most inclined to pray when we are alone with our thoughts. That happens often in our hurry-up-and-wait world: we're busy, but we're alone. However, God is always there, and so those times are some of the best to pray.

Prayer is not a memorized verse (although it could be if that's what you desire). The prayer I'm talking about is simply good, decent, thoughts and words said privately.

Prayer can also be random acts of kindness: a wordy way of saying *consideration*. Consideration is giving thoughtful attention to others, the kind we wish others would give us. It's helping someone who is struggling, either with a particular situation or with life in general.

Let's say you see a kid running down the hall at school with books falling everywhere, trying to make it to class on time. Take two seconds to look in his eyes with understanding, then pick up his books for him and smile. Mission accomplished!

Maybe at lunch there's a new girl who can't speak English and you can't speak her language. But hey, you can communicate with your eyes and by sharing your candy bar. Your actions say it all.

In both cases, you've been considerate. You've done for others what you would want done for you. Call it service, random acts of kindness, consideration, even prayer: it creates happiness for you and others.

Look Above.
Look in the
Mirror.

173

The Power of Prayer

When you feel as though the whole world is coming down on you—and that happens periodically in everyone's life—prayer in any of its forms can give you a sense of peace, of stability and security.

When I was fourteen, I felt as though my world was caving in. For some reason (I don't even recall specifics now) I ran away from home. I was walking to my girlfriend's because she said I could stay there that night, when I spotted our Church in the distance and—at the very same moment—my mom in our VW bus, already out looking for me. However, I wasn't ready to go home yet, so I dropped to my belly, and did an army crawl across an open field to get to our Church. I needed that sense of peace I knew I'd find there, the security to reflect and size up my situation. Even then, prayer acted as a quality sounding board for me.

No, prayer doesn't take away the pain and make it all better, but it does give you a short breather, and hope for happier days.

What about when you face the absolutely worst catastrophes? The kind of ugly fate where you ask yourself over and over again, "Why me?" When you've cried so long that your tears are all dried up, and you wish they weren't, because your sorrow is far from over, and you must have a way to express it. Is prayer really going to make any difference?

Yes.

*Sex, Boys
& You:
Be Your
Own Best
Girlfriend*

174

All those years ago when Church was my refuge, when I prayed, "Please, dear Jesus, make it stop, make That Boy go away," and yet it didn't stop and he didn't go away—even then I never gave up and I never stopped believing that one day I would find happiness.

Prayer gave me the courage to withstand and go on. Finally, when I was ten years old, prayer gave me the courage to tell my parents about the abuse. Fortunately, they believed me. That was the turning point in my young life. Prayer was the instrument that gave me the strength, the power, the courage to reach that point and make it happen.

Whether or not you pray is your decision. But, I can tell you from my own experience that failing to connect with that Higher Being puts you deeper into a dungeon of despair. The black hole, as you know from experience, gets you nowhere.

I'm asking you to believe, as I do, with your whole heart and soul, that you can rise above your problems and connect with Goodness. If you look, and God knows you have to look hard sometimes, Light prevails, even if it is just a lightening of your spirit.

The Window of Your Soul

During the Middle Ages, people believed that the eyes were windows into the soul. And they were right, so very right, all those years ago.

Up until now, you may have only used your mirror to see how you look. Start using it to see how you *are.* Focus on your eyes, only your eyes; allow the rest of your image to fade into the backdrop, and pierce through to what's really important, the truth of what you feel and think.

Have you ever done this? Have you ever noticed how your eyes speak a thousand words, even if you never open your mouth. If you haven't, you may find it's quite frightening at first, almost eerie. But, you need to do it.

You know how you don't want to make eye contact with someone when you've done something wrong or been

Look Above.
Look in the
Mirror.

mischievous? Or, when you've lied or disappointed someone? If they finally get you to make eye contact, you hardly have to say a word: your eyes speak for you.

Your eyes speak to you, too, if you let them. They tell you you're sad, even though you're desperately staying busy to avoid facing that sadness. Your eyes tell you when you're tired, discouraged, or doing things that run counter to your dreams.

But, your eyes can do even more.

Tell Yourself, "Yes, I Can"

Whenever my girls and I watch ice skaters on television, we see each one, right before his/her appearance, receiving a last-minute pep talk from their coach. Without fail, each coach delivers a talk while looking their student straight in the eye. That coach wants to know exactly what their skater is thinking, so they can choose the perfect words to motivate and instill confidence.

You can do that for yourself. Simply by looking in the mirror and engaging in some positive self-talk. It may sound goofy, but it works. Stand in front of your mirror, look yourself in the eye, and have a good long chat with yourself *out loud* (I am assuming you'll try this alone; try this in public and you may get some pretty strange reactions.)

Use only the most positive words in your vocabulary. Ask questions if you like, but respond with only direct, self-assured answers.

Maybe you'll ask yourself how you want others to perceive you today: be incredibly descriptive when you answer. "I want other people to think I'm strong, intelligent,

*Sex, Boys
& You:
Be Your
Own Best
Girlfriend*

176

charismatic, irresistible and amazing." Speak it out loud, with drama and conviction in your voice. Repeat it until it catches hold in your soul, your mind, and your body, and you believe it with every fiber of your being.

Perhaps you want to hurdle a fear. Tell yourself—out loud—that you will no longer *allow* yourself to be afraid or shy. Start with "I cans" and "I wills."

This is self-affirmation. Look into your eyes and first convince yourself. And then you go out and convince the world.

So, face that mirror every day, and listen to what your eyes are telling you. If you don't like what they're saying, change them. Fill them with dreams that sparkle, and with love, so that when they talk, they tell everyone around you that you're kind, strong, giving, and powerful. Let your eyes say that you've given yourself permission to receive the best from life, and that when you do, you want to share it with others.

You Get What You Ask For

My best friend is overweight. In our current culture, many people regard obesity as nearly criminal behavior, just a step or two above committing ax murders. But my dear, sweet friend has encountered little prejudice and discrimination in her life, although she's large.

Do you know why? Because she never expects to be treated badly. Look into her eyes and they say, "I'm a person of worth. Respect me." She backs that up by being an excellent businesswoman and of service to all around her. Whenever we are together, I am amazed at her magnetism: people are drawn to her like bees to honey. There's no sign in her eyes

Look Above.
Look in the
Mirror.

that says "I'm fat: kick me." Instead, my friend gets back exactly what she puts out—it's a boomerang effect.

If you're not happy, ask yourself two questions: *What am I thinking? What am I doing for others?* Then go to the mirror for the answers.

If your eyes tell you that you aren't thinking positively, if you're dwelling on all the garbage in life, you're not going to be happy and you're certainly not going to spread much happiness around. So, make a choice to *think about what you think.*

What you do speaks so loudly I cannot hear what you say.

– Ralph Waldo Emerson

Are your thought patterns a constant downer? Then I don't care if you've got a hot body, the coolest guy in school panting after you, have super grades, and are part of the in crowd. Those unhappy thoughts are going to make you unhappy, and they're going to try to infect everyone around you. How do you think those folks will treat you in return?

Always remember that you set the tone for your life. The pace. The pattern. In most cases, others will take your lead if it's set with conviction and kindness. In that sense, you exercise a tremendous amount of power over what you *allow* in your life.

You may not realize you're being negative or allowing others to treat you badly. But, the second you take a look in the mirror and realize what's going on, you must stop it dead in its tracks. Your life is like a film: you are the director, you own the director's chair, and no one—absolutely no one—has the privilege of sitting in that seat but you!

Attitude is Everything

Short and sweet, what I'm talking about is attitude. A positive attitude is the ticket to life. Once you've got it, treasure it, keep it safe—heck, laminate it if you can figure out how—so that it can never become tattered or defaced.

Attitude is one thing in life that can never be taken from you. It's part of your personal style. Attitude is more important than money, jobs, education, possessions, relationships, even the roof over our heads. It can make a house a home, unite a family, and make friendship a true communion of spirits.

Attitude makes things happen. I know, because it did for me.

When I gave up my bad attitudes and self-defeating thinking, I also locked up my past, threw it down a deep, dark hole, and tossed away the key forever. Then I really started to live. I began to pursue my dreams, full speed ahead. I took a look at what was good and right about me, and, in turn, I began to draw out what was good and right in everyone around me. It didn't all happen at once: as you know, my journey took a long, long time, and in many ways, it continues still.

The little girl who could never smile became a kind, strong, giving, powerful woman who rarely stops smiling. The ugly duckling who was shy and awkward came to understand that she was beautiful, not just because she learned what made her look good on the outside, but because she developed the potential for loveliness that resides in all our souls, namely that inner beauty that causes our outer edge to radiate life.

Look Above.
Look in the
Mirror.

Yes, They Work

I know I risk sounding idealistic—maybe even silly to some—when I talk about looking in the mirror or looking above to a Higher Power.

But, it works.

After all, belief in your beliefs and belief in yourself is all you have. Nobody can take those things away from you: turning inward and upward can strengthen both.

So, look inside, where you can see the real you. And pray, because your prayer is yours alone. Do both faithfully, and you'll never lack the strength and determination to stay on the path to your dreams, and be your own best girlfriend.

The Happiness Creed

A MILLENNIUM APPROACH TO PRAYER

Think about what you think.
Because good thoughts create good actions.
Good actions create great responses—
Responses that mirror what you've given.
That is the truth.
Like it. Hate it. Or believe it.

And if the truth hurts,
Make a choice to first change the reflection you see in your mirror.
For there begins your happiness, which only you can make.
You're happy. Everybody's happy.
Then service is effortless.
Prayer ubiquitous.
Happiness, the high plane upon which you choose to live.

— Joni Arredia

Look Above.
Look in the
Mirror.

Epilogue

My dear young friends,

Your muliebrity is what you are born with as a baby girl.
Now is the time in your life—your teenage years—to
enhance it and learn to mold it into whatever shape you
desire. Learn this at your young age so that you can be giant
steps ahead of where generations of women before you have
been.

Learn that your woman's intuition is among your strongest
qualities. Discover that your ability to nurture and sacrifice,
if given freely, helps others find the very best part of
themselves. Realize that discipline is your greatest ally in
achieving your dreams. Know that you are strong, and that
as a woman you set the tone for a situation, a home, a
relationship, a business, a life. But, only if you have the
confidence in yourself to do so.

As you follow the path to your dreams, write me and let me
know how you're doing. I really do care about you, and I
love getting mail.

All my love,

Joni

Perc Publishing, Inc.
P.O. Box 351030
Toledo, OH 43635

The Doodlers

My sincere and loving thanks go to the students in Mr. Steve Wipfli's Junior High art class at Ottawa Hills High School in Toledo, Ohio in the spring of 1998, and to the others whose candid works on bits of paper embellish these pages: Melissa Cote-Hooven, Kelly Creech, Tracy Curtis, Kevin Ewing, Candace Hallauer, Julia Masters, Niko Ormond, Meg Price, Ashley Redmann, Liz Sammons, Annie Valusna, Sarah Vitale, Marlene Yousif, and Danny Zangara.

The author as seen through the eyes of her daughters

Out of the mouths of babes!

Lauren:

My mom…what can I say…she's my angel. My Mom would put anything aside just to help others because of her love of people. She has a heart of gold which she uses to motivate other people to follow their hearts. My Mom's hard drive keeps her strong through the good and bad times. To me she is a brilliant person who makes me want to strive for the best in everything. I love my Mom with all my soul and I am very proud of all she's accomplished.

Emily:

Joni Arredia is a wonderful speaker and writer. Many women and girls look up to her for her always cheerful, get up and get going kind of ways. Not only for those reasons though, she speaks out for many women and girls that need self-esteem. I don't look up to her just for those reasons, but she is also my Mother. I am writing this biography, with no editors mind you, because my sister and I are about the age she is shooting for to read this book. My name is Emily and I am thirteen years old, and my sister Lauren is eighteen. Of course, having her as my Mom isn't all fun and games. We have our fights just like you and your Mom, but it can also be lots of fun. She is writing this book to make sure you LOVE yourself, which is part of being a woman. My Mom says just the right things to make you feel warm inside. She can give answers to some questions you also might have. As Mom would say, be kind, strong, giving, and powerful and all your dreams will come true.

FROM LEFT: Lauren, Joni, and Emily Arredia.

An enormous thank you to Stone Bland, a Perfect Stranger/Perfect Friend. We had never met before, and yet she was kind enough to ride her beautiful Harley, Midnight Rider, out to the site of the photo shoot for for us to use as a backdrop prop. Stone waited patiently, encouraging us with her smiles. It was the first time the three Arredia girls had the pleasure of sitting on a Harley Davidson motorcycle!

PERC stands for PERSONAL ENERGIES, RESOURCES, AND CAPABILITIES.

Perhaps you have someone dear in mind who you know would enjoy the messages in our publications. We hope you'll take this opportunity to order one of the following items for her benefit. Please feel free to contact us at any hour, any day, at the following numbers:

TOLL-FREE PHONE ORDERS AND CUSTOMER SERVICE
1-888-GET-PERC (1-888-438-7372)

TOLL-FREE FAX ORDERS
1-800-286-6212

If one of the items you are ordering is a gift, we'd be happy to simplify the gift-giving process for you. When you order, be sure to include the name and address of that lucky person along with a few words straight from your heart. We'll enclose a gift card with the chosen item(s), and ship it directly to your Perfect Friend(s).

Please know that a shipping and handling charge will be added to your order total. In addition, the required sales tax will be added for Ohio residents. We can accept VISA, MasterCard, American Express, and Discover. Sorry, no checks.

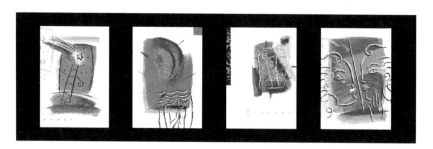

Joni's Write Stuff
Colorful high gloss notecards featuring illustrations and thoughts from Joni. Set of 12 cards in four bold designs with inspiring quotes and additional colorful designs on the back. Includes matching envelopes. $18.95

Muliebrity: Qualities of a Woman
BOOK

"If you want to master the qualities of being a woman with confidence, verve and vitality, read this book."

– Mark Victor Hansen, co-author, New York Times #1 Best Selling **Chicken Soup for the Soul** series

192 pages of inspiration and motivation; hardcover; illustrated. $17.95

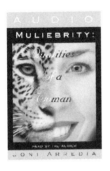

Muliebrity: Qualities of a Woman
AUDIOBOOK

Full version of the book, read by Joni. Three tapes, runs approximately 3½ hours. $17.95

Sex, Boys & You: Be Your Own Best Girlfriend
BOOK

192 pages of inspiring common sense advice and shared life experiences for teenage girls; quality softcover; illustrated. $15.95

Perc Presentation

Joni's favorite thing is to motivate people! Invite her to speak with your company, organization, or school. Contact customer service or fax her directly at 419-531-8866.

Perc Publishing

P.O. BOX 351030 • TOLEDO, OHIO 43635 • 1-888-GET-PERC